The Last Anglo-Indians

THE STORY OF A MIDDLE-CLASS ANGLO-INDIAN FAMILY IN INDIA

A biographical account of events from the 1880s to 1950s

SONINA K. MATTEO

Tech Research Services Publishing
www.techresearchservices.com

These are biographical vignettes spanning 3 generations. In some cases the names and circumstances of particular people were changed, but the story is essentially correct.

Contributor – Yvonne Velasquez (nee LeStyne)
Photographic credits are provided in the Appendix. All other photographs are from the author's family collection.
Only a portion of the family tree is published here.

Library of Congress Cataloging-in-Publication Data

Includes bibliographical references

eBook
ISBN-10:0578162296
ISBN-13:978-0-578-16229-4

Print Book
ISBN-10:0578158841
ISBN-13:978-0-578-15884-6

Dedicated to my mother Yvonne

PROLOGUE

This story is neither an attempt at the social history of Anglo-India, nor an analysis of colonial regression, but a story that draws on many noteworthy historical events at various points within an Anglo-Indian family. It is my goal to bring out the story of three generations during the late 19th century into the 20th century in British India: two separate grandmothers (one who refused to embrace India and one that did), and a mother and her daughter. Their experiences allow us to understand the ways in which British colonial views of relationships and setting, both conditioned and are conditioned by the perceptions of the various people who inhabit the landscape.

It was in Calcutta that the young 16-year old Anglo-Indian girl, Dolly Devereux ran away from her mother's home and fled to the growing town of Lahore in Northern India.

Eurasians in India, known as the Anglo Indians, were at a cultural crossroads at the wake of the 20th century. Pure-blooded Indians disregarded them, and the British looked down on them as not being British enough. Being all of 16 years old in the early 1900s, Dolly faced an uncertain future after running away from her English family. Were her future and dreams forever gone, or was this going to be the start of a better life?

After meeting James, the son of the Superintendant of the India Telephone and Telegraph, she fell in love and married him. Soon, she and her new family found themselves in Poona. The "Monsoon Capital" as Poona was known, served as the military garrison for the British Army. It was here that James was lucky enough to find work at an Armory during the height of the Depression. As the story unfolds, we see the progress and development of middle-class Anglo-Indian institutions, which were always marked by a blend of both traditions from the East and the West.

Early on, many Anglo Indians would believe themselves to be above the pure blooded Indian race, often speaking down to the native Indians and about going back "home" to England. They held a fascination for the monarchy and everything British. We also see some of the obstacles the average middle-class Anglo-Indian family faced and their attempts at embracing the new and changing India.

This story provides a glimpse of what happened to middle-class Anglo-Indians in India and how the quest for the country's Independence caused a mass exodus of Anglo-Indians in the 1940s and 1950s.

FOREWORD TO MY RELATIVES

The process that has been used to uncover this story was derived from 3 sources: conversations with my mother, talks with her family and friends, and historical research.

This is somewhat of a memoir of my mother's life in India. My objective is to inform, enlighten and raise the curiosity of the audience as I highlight the high points of her life there. They are moments that were important and interesting to her—showing the people, places and events that shaped her life in India, then her life before leaving India for America, which was at the time of the first phase of immigration after Indian Independence.

This biographical adaptation of Yvonne's direct ancestry line could be considered a novelization of events. It was written with the hope that it will give you, your children and future relatives a better understanding of your roots. I have tried to describe the life of her former days so that you may feel a part of them. Even more, I have wished to make your ancestors come to life as real people, for you to understand the joys and sorrows of everyday life.

In some cases the names and circumstances of particular people were changed, but their stories are essentially true.

Researching and writing this has been a rewarding experience and I hope you will enjoy it.

I thank my mother for the writing challenge, and the legacy she and our Anglo-Indian ancestors left us to remember.

With love, Sonina

TABLE OF CONTENTS

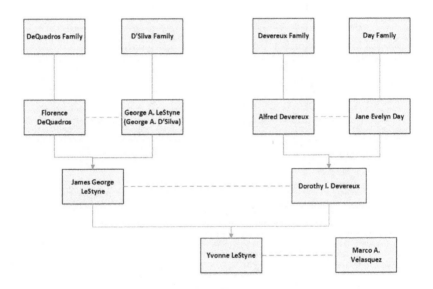

Evelyn Meets Alfred in Calcutta

In the 19th century, Calcutta's Port was the premier port in British India. It *was* the port of entry.

Europeans, Asians, Africans and more were allowed to pass through the port bringing merchandise by water or land, into and out of the country. But Calcutta was not only a port city; it was the capital of India. All the ships from abroad and throughout India came to Calcutta's port bringing food, clothes, furniture, machines, and friends, workers, and relatives of all races.

British policy during the 19th Century was mainly concerned with expanding and protecting its hold on Indian resources. India was viewed as its most valuable colony. Seeing an opportunity to be in the right place at the right time and great promise for stable military work in Calcutta, the Day family had made the decision to leave England and start a temporary home in Calcutta. They were drawn for economic reasons, but also by the mystery and beauty of the East. When in India, they saw opportunity and took hold of it, exhibiting their sensibility to change in many different ways. Anyone walking into their family bungalow could tell, from the way the rooms were furnished that they were entering an English household. The rooms were packed with upholstered armchairs, elaborate cabinetry, and grandiose draperies. The English home there was typically a rented house or large flat. The English family in

India was aware of their superior standing and expected those around them to notice. Although in Mrs. Day's ancestry there was a struggle to get from Ireland to England, all that remained really of their pride for Ireland was an occasional Irish stew, which their oldest daughter Jane Evelyn enjoyed to watch being prepared, and then eat every time her mother's servant made it.

At the time when the Days considered this migration to the Southeast, British military tactics were changing in India. The British government directly managed India on its own land, but after Indian uprisings and war, it decided on a different approach in colonial government to rule *through* the Indian upper classes rather than in opposition to them.

Settling in India was a challenging decision for Evelyn's family, but they felt they needed to go. There were military tasks that needed to be done and her father was in the military. Duty called. They settled in Calcutta when their daughter Evelyn was still not yet married, but a young girl filled with obedience and loyalty to her parents.

In 1885 her parents' friends were living comfortably drawing a salary from the military or other profession. A few of them managed Indian human resources in the textile industries, while others were in the Jute industries. Whilst in India, they were not rich, but upper-middle class, mingling occasionally with the elite at social clubs and parties.

At night, Evelyn listened to her parents' conversations, as they undressed after an evening's party or dinner. She was able to crouch down on the stairs and hear them above the clatter of the servants cleaning the kitchen.

"When will we be able to get back to England? It is just ghastly here. I'm sick of the conversation and people," Evelyn's mother said. "Let's, go back," she pleaded with her husband.

"Yes, did you see that Mr. Corey, put a serviette around his neck? *Ghastly*," said Evelyn's father.

"But dear, the voyage back by boat would be more than 4 weeks. We can't keep going back and forth," Evelyn's father said. "We must stay here until I finish my duty in the military."

"I don't like these people they call Eurasians or Anglo-Indians. They treat us as though we are equals. When a middle-aged woman is so dark that she looks like she should be in Black Town and puts on such airs, it is alarming," said Evelyn's mother.

There were two distinctive towns in Calcutta at that time: White Town, which was primarily British and near the business district of Chowringhee, and then there was Black Town, mainly Indian and close to Northern Calcutta. Evelyn and her family lived in White Town.

At 16, Evelyn was attending private school and enjoying her life in India regardless of how her family saw things. She did not share her parents' view entirely that England's way of life was the more civilized. Although she did think that the English were the superior race, as she was brought up that way, within her circle of friends, life here in India was what was normal for her. She attended boarding school in India and learned music, cooking and sewing among British teachers and mentors. Fashion was very important to her. She wore her bodice in the youthful style—very tight fitted as a result of darts and princess seams. She wore clothes with dropped waists to make it seem she had a very long torso. Her collars were always very high. She loved the look of the corseted silhouette, with a simpler skirt suited for riding, a tall shirt collar, and a feathered hat. And, with her friends she started to frequent the military functions wearing skirts just above her ankles. And on a fateful night, dressed in her favorite corseted dress and feathered hat, at just such a military function she met Alfred Devereux.

In this year of 1885, Alfred Devereux was an engineer on board a naval ship. He was stationed in Calcutta. His parents R. and A. Devereux, who were from families of good-standing in British society, remained at his childhood home in England, as did Alfred's heart. And so, every few months he traveled back and forth from the port of Calcutta to England to see his parents. In England, he relaxed with his parents and friends from University and military school for a few days. He loved to be home in England and everyday longed to return. He endured hot, humid India as it was his duty and offered a solid, stable income, but he longed for a life where he would be back again in England with conversations full of substance, with his fellow university buddies, and cool crisp nights instead of hot steamy ones filled with biting mosquitoes. But he knew that he had more years ahead of him to serve his mother country. With all his ambivalence for India, he managed to face each day with a smile and obedience. The work was interesting for him and challenging. The challenge and the salary were the only things that made him want to stay. He knew the Indian empire was of highest importance, but the people around him were so foreign and so very different, he could not help but feel that he was in their territory and didn't belong.

Lately, after reading the world news, waves of uneasiness would wash over him. He grew up hearing great things about India. Therefore he made the move to this foreign land with hope and excitement. His boyhood images of this land were shifting in his mind. After years in India he had a different perspective. The original images were from a magnificent past---a departing past. He could not stop feeling that a storm was coming in the future.

When Alfred and Evelyn's parents lived their lives in India in the 1870s, the British Empire was powerful and entrenched around the world. The expansion of the British Empire created the consequences of worldwide industrialization and urbanization. This had its impact on the middle class, of which Evelyn's grandparents were a part. In the UK and throughout the British Empire ideas of economic individualism, Laissez-faire government, free competition and free trade had already surfaced and were understood and accepted as the norm. However, the competition between large economic powers throughout Europe and the worldwide marketplace had affected not only relationships with each country, but also with those less-developed areas upon which they were increasingly dependent for raw materials. Such areas included India, Africa and China.

Throughout Europe, liberalism was on the rise through the 1870s. With liberalism came an idea that there should be a government in place in which the interests of the natives would be protected by direct representatives of the population. The idea also included a belief in a foreign policy based on peace and free trade. Many middle class Anglo-Indian men and women shared these beliefs and worked hard to carry through these principles in every day life.

As mentioned before, in the 1880s the British government directly managed India, but after earlier Indian uprisings and war, they decided to rule India through the Indian upper classes rather than in opposition to them. Indian customs were tolerated as they had not been before, and princes and bureaucracies were incorporated as protectorates into the general scheme of government.

Back in England, Alfred's parents were keenly interested in these changes. They carefully read the newspapers, about how around 1885, Calcutta was hosting the first national conference of the Indian National Association.[1] Soon afterward they read of even more revolutionary organizations associated with the Indian independence movement. Robert Devereux urged his son Alfred to be careful, and even to leave this post, saying "it will likely affect you directly". But Alfred did not want to leave yet. He insisted on staying in India and finishing off his military duty.

So, it was in this political climate, while carrying out his post as a Naval Ship engineer in Calcutta, at one of the naval dances, that Alfred was introduced to Jane Evelyn Day. "They call me Evelyn". She would eventually look into his eyes, gently take his hand and smile. She would whisper to all her friends afterwards that she thought him very gallant and polite. While, he saw something as well in her--that she was strong and a woman full of life. She would come to know through friendly conversations that he was of good standing within the military and the community. This was important to her, because she knew it would be important to her family.

Within months Alfred asked for Evelyn's hand in marriage. Her parents were overjoyed to hear that this young, strapping man with an excellent position and family in the English society within India was engaged to their daughter.

Soon after, at a dinner in which all were invited, Evelyn's father was the first to voice his concerns about what the political climate would mean for Evelyn and Alfred.

"You know this isn't the 1820s when the Brits experienced great prosperity here. Those were days of great influence for our community. There was little discrimination between Brits and Indians then. That's not the case today. You, my dear man, were taken freely into the covenant ranks of the British services and reached a high position of trust and responsibility," said Mr. Day to Alfred over the candelabras and fine china.

Mrs. Day added, "Yes, this community is drawn mostly from those professional soldiers and military adventurers." She smiled at the young man in front of her. "What we are trying to say Alfred, is that this India is no longer that India."

"We understand mother," said Evelyn.

"We just want you to understand what a challenge it will be to bring up your children here. We want you to consider going back to England right away."

Alfred and Evelyn glanced at each other and took a deep breadth. "We understand your concern," started Alfred. "The British are leading from a separate place, far away. That is the issue. We see that the Anglo-Indians, who we are both friends with now and are ingrained in our community, are not respected by the Brits and really never were. And now, our services of building telegraphs and railways, are really just seen in a subordinate capacity as well," said Alfred to his future in-laws.

When they finished dinner and they were alone again, he heeded Mr. Day's words and tried to soothe Evelyn's mind. "It will be hard, but I'm sure we can do it," said Alfred to his beloved Evelyn.

Evelyn and Alfred eventually married and settled in Calcutta. As the years went by, they saw the entire city grow around them. Alfred worked long days and sometimes needed to stay away for weeks. He missed his family greatly when away. He sent money home to Evelyn to maintain their modest home.

In the meantime, she stayed at home providing Alfred with sons, then a daughter. As the family grew, they planned for their education: the dilemma always being –in India or back in England.

British sponsored schools in India continued in English. Thomas Babington Macaulay, a well-respected British Statesman had long ago proposed a British education regime and ideology for India, followed by the English *Education Act of 1835*, together these would groom brown-skinned natives into English men (Anglo-Indians). A new group of westernized and nationalistic loyal Indian civil servants and businessmen thus emerged by the end of the nineteenth century, trained by the British.[2]

Nightly, Alfred returned from the ship to see Evelyn and—first Jack, then Stanley, and then Dorothy and two others followed. They managed with hard-working, loyal servants helping them maintain a stable life in the hot Indian summers and monsoon months.

Their friends commented on the Devereux' strong union and how their children were likely on their way to the best private boarding schools and careers that British India had to offer.

Alfred and his peers read newspapers to understand the latest current events happening in Mother Country, England, and the latest news of the war throughout the world.

When WWI broke out in 1914, India was in a state of growing political unrest. The Indian National Congress had gone from being a group that simply discussed issues to a body that was pushing for more self-government.[3] Before the war started, the Germans had spent a great deal of time and energy trying to stir up an anti-British movement in India. Many shared the view that if Britain got involved in a crisis somewhere in the world, Indian separatists would use this as an opportunity to advance their cause. These fears were unfounded. When war was started, all of India rallied to the cause—natives, Anglo-Indians, and Eurasians aligning with Britain. But the strain of the First World War was driving Alfred and his friends and family to rethink where they wanted to live and be. The pressure from family, friends and work were mounting for Alfred.

It was early one October morning when the servant woke Evelyn in her chambers. "Is Mr. Devereux awake?" Evelyn asked.

"No, Madam, still asleep,"

She left Alfred still in his bed asleep. It had been a long time since she had slept longer than him. It was midmorning, after the children were in school and the other beds made, before she returned to check on him, thinking what the servants will say about her husband languishing in the room for half the day.

When she approached his bed, she noticed his look was faintly odd and the smell was different. It was about 1 minute later before she realized something was terribly wrong. She screamed out in horror. All the servants came running. The rest of the day was a blur for her. It was still relatively warm out, but not sweltering on that day in 1922 when her husband Alfred Devereux died of a heart attack at the young age of 57. For Evelyn, life was hard to bear from the beginning—facing a lack of support and a lack of money. It was beyond a sense of sadness, but more hopelessness. Her husband gone now, Evelyn was left a widow at 53 with 5 children at her side.

Dorothy (Dolly) and her brothers were called home from school and brought into the living room immediately to be told. The news was devastating on so many levels for everyone in the family. Dolly's father, Alfred was the provider and the emotional anchor for them all.

Dolly had enjoyed 12 years with her father in Calcutta before his death. Every word and every memory of him she thought back on was a good one. But to share that with her mother was not possible. Her mother was "too conservative for that", Dolly thought, and her brothers were also not accessible or open as well. It was not the English way to be so emotional. She longed for someone to share her anguish with.

Dolly was heart broken by her father's death and mourned him at times, and in a way, that her mother never knew about. Dolly grew into adolescence, while her mother still never shared her feelings of sadness over the loss of her husband, Dolly's father. Evelyn would only talk to Dolly to tell her what to wear, what to do, and what to say.

As the years went on and she grew to be a young, beautiful teenager, she could think of nothing but wanting to be free of her mother and other guardians and all the authoritative commands she heard daily. All she wanted to do was to see her friends, attend dances and parties and connect with those who understood her.

Meanwhile Dolly's mother, Evelyn had other things on her mind. She was finding it increasingly difficult to manage her existing lifestyle in British India alone with 5 children. She decided it was time to remarry. It was then that she was introduced to John Rixson by a friend in the Anglo-Indian military. Although younger than her, she seized the opportunity and reasoned to herself that she was at a good age *now* to marry this man. Initially, she didn't think him a good match because he was 10 years younger than her and the age difference would be hard for him as well as her.

John Rixson was a long standing bachelor and military man. He had a hard time adjusting to marrying a woman with children. He realized the benefits the action bestowed, as his new wife would get her late husband's pension from the British government. Also, she was a well respected, level-headed society woman, who also had some footing in England. John felt in his heart that he was British—it was his mother country and Evelyn was of British descent, and a smart, honest and loyal woman. "She would do fine as my wife," Rixson told his friends.

Evelyn sought out Mr. Baban, her chief Indian servant, asking him to arrange for Mr. Rixson to meet the rest of the servants whenever it was convenient.

Between the many visits from friends and relatives and Rixson's continual conversation with her over the months, he had a fair grasp of how the home was arranged and who did what, when. Structurally, the home was a comfortable bungalow, built in the late 1850s. It had been renovated to include a conservatory and somewhat formal dining room on the first floor and guest quarters in the back.

The brick home was almost a complete rectangle with a section cut out for the inner courtyard. Cobblestones below, toward the entrance of every doorway led to the relaxing, sunstroked area in the center. Once there, you can see and hear almost everything that was going on.

The conservatory had wide windows, allowing breathtaking views of the Indian countryside.

In the early 1910s, more money was being pumped into the Calcutta infrastructure, including the telegraph and Howrah railway, so the landscape was dotted with more commercial buildings and fewer acres of farm land as the years went on.

In the weeks following the engagement, John and widowed Evelyn spoke about their future. She no longer had the income coming in as she did before. She had to face it that with 5 kids and her new husband's military salary they would need to live more modestly and with just a minimum of Indian servants. Returning to England now was not an option, as her fiancé was stationed in the armed forces there in India.

He talked of his duties at work frequently, to the point where she understood much of what he did. She felt secure with him and soon felt that her decision was a good one. She grew to be very protective of John and his reputation. She did not want anything happening to him as it did to her first husband. No illness, no trouble. She did not want any more drama in her life, and knew that no other man would marry her with 5 kids and as old as she was.

Eventually the marriage took place. Evelyn married John Rixson in a small ceremony in Calcutta. She used Devereux-Rixson as her surname, holding the well-to-do Devereux name and Rixson to show others that she was remarried and aligned again with another.

Dolly's Decision

The challenge for Evelyn was her teenage daughter Dorothy. Dolly, as everyone called her, was in her teenage years, and Evelyn found her very difficult to manage. She didn't know what to do with her after seeing her young and different attitude.

John saw Dolly a few times every week, and was noticing her growing up in front of him. Because he didn't have a sister, he had never been this close to a young teenage girl. He saw how vulnerable and innocent she was, yet headstrong she could be.

It was midweek, and Evelyn had gotten up unusually early. She was leaving the bathroom when she glanced around to see her husband leaning against the doorway, arms crossed and eyes lazily exploring her daughter's body from across the hall. The door to Dolly's room was ajar.

"Dolly, please close your door when you are getting ready for school," said Evelyn.

Evelyn could not help but be very jealous of her daughter around her new husband. He was so much younger than her and very handsome. Dolly was 16 years old when arguments escalated between her and her Mum. Dolly tried to make things right in subtle ways like asking the cook to prepare meals for the newlyweds, and handling some of their chores, but whatever she did, it was not good enough and "Mum was never really happy".

Evelyn made sure the servants, or one of Dolly's brothers was always there while she was out. "Why, Mum?" asked Jack.

"I just don't want to leave them alone," Evelyn said one day to her son. And she never did. She never allowed Dolly to be alone in the house with her husband.

A fear grew month after month in Evelyn. Before long she could even voice it to herself. She was afraid that her husband would fall in love with her daughter, and she would lose another husband.

After a fight with her mother, Dolly found solace in her room with maps of India and the world. She longed to travel and kept no secret of it. India was one of the larger countries located in Southeast Asia, with a total land area of 3.3 million square km and millions of people. It was the jewel of the British crown. It was divided into 28 states plus the capital, which eventually became Delhi. She could think of nothing else but exploring it.

In 1905, the province of Bengal was partitioned apart from Calcutta along communal lines. This resulted in what Evelyn and John remembered as widespread public anxiety and a boycott of British goods. These activities, along with the disadvantageous location of Calcutta on the eastern fringes of India, prompted the British to move the capital north to Delhi in 1911 (now New Delhi).[4]

Delhi was a city dotted with ancient monuments and now was becoming a city of new building infrastructure for future growth. The city offered religious diversity, yet retained the essence of each culture the ancient Indian, the Mughal, and the British. Restaurants and retail stores grew. One could easily find a good meal for 1 rupee to 100 rupees. Beautiful gardens provided opportunity for leisurely walks located steps away from busy political and business corridors. The population grew exponentially around Delhi and other northern Indian cities, especially with the younger generation of Anglo Indians looking for jobs.

Dorothy's home was in India. She was a person of British descent, born and living in India. She was known to some as Eurasian, while to herself and others, she was Anglo-Indian.

In 1927, Dorothy Devereux (Dolly) at 16-years old decided to run away from home and move with her girlfriend Lobo DeSouza and her family in Lahore, India.

Before the partition, Lahore belonged to Punjab British India. There, in every sight and sound, the ancestry of the Mughals lived. Dolly and her friends took rides around visiting the great Badshahi mosque, one of the city's major tourist areas. Badshahi was a sign of grandeur in the Mughal times and had majestic features people revered. They would often see people going in or coming out of the mosque and surrounding grounds to pray. As the girls were all British Catholics, they did not dare go inside, but watched always from afar.

By early 1928, when she and her friend settled in a small flat in Lahore, Dolly met James LeStyne. James LeStyne, another Anglo Indian, was living in a flat upstairs and Dolly downstairs with Lobo in a small building on Gray Street, when James was invited for tea. James LeStyne was a darker Anglo Indian with relatives having roots going further back in India. His Mom's side was from Goa and his father's side elsewhere. Both had mixed European and Indian descent.

Tea turned into other social invitations. Social gatherings and trips with friends turned into outings for the twosome and more tea near Chief's college and then Anarkali Gardens. Before long, she fell in love with his cool brown eyes and light brown skin.

James adored her. He started courting her persistently. They soon began attending Anglo Indian functions and Dorothy was said to be "with James". She didn't care how Indian he looked. She would be his. They fell in love with each other's bright warm smiles under the cool northern Indian skies.

They married with friends all around on a hot and rainy August day in 1928 in Lahore, India. Dolly's mother Evelyn Devereux and John Rixson did not attend.

"You are asking for trouble marrying this dark Indian," Evelyn said to her daughter when she heard of the news. "If you do this, you are no longer alive to us."

Dolly's mother Evelyn refused to go to her daughter's wedding. She still did not reconcile after they parted ways and now this marriage to a darker Anglo-Indian went further against her English tolerance.

James worked at the telegraph, as did many Anglo Indians at the time. His father, the Superintendent of the Telegraph helped him acquire the coveted job. He spoke English very well with little or no Indian accent. James knew that was important, as these places did not hire just any Anglo-Indian, but Anglo-Indians that spoke British-English very well. Also, he did not want to embarrass his father, who had a prominent position within the company, so he always tried to refine his speech and educate himself.

In the meantime, railways and railway bridges were being erected all around the world—in Paris, New York, and London. Increased consumption of manufactured goods, including cars was being seen throughout India. Sewing machines were being used by Anglo-Indian and Indian women to create new fashions. A new capitalism was abounding in this ancient land.

James had a job opportunity on the railway, another service owned and operated by the British, but he saw more opportunity at the telegraph since his dad held a secure position as the Superintendent.

He did not say I love you every time he came back from work, but Dolly and James took solace in gazing into each other's eyes and sharing a few tender words and sometimes writing love letters.

Dolly so loved James that she would do anything for him. As time went on, if it were even possible, she grew even more attached to and in love with him. When he was away, she was always uneasy and never content.

The Great Depression
Hits India

The Great Depression in India had a tumultuous effect on the British-run India. The British-run Indian government adopted a trade policy to safeguard itself against economic losses. It proved positive to the United Kingdom, but caused immense harm to the Indian economy. From 1929–1937, exports and imports fell dramatically causing seaborne international trade to slow to a near standstill, considerably affecting ports like Calcutta and Bombay—cities at the heart of Indian commerce.

The railways and the agricultural sector were the most affected. Due to a decline in exports and imports, and thereby, in the transportation of goods, the railway revenues decreased. James and Dolly's friends in those sectors lost jobs and started moving away to cities that offered other or better opportunities. Some started moving back to England.

During this time, India's share of world income started falling dramatically (from a once 25% in the 1700s, to below 5% in the 1950s). India's per-capita income for the year 1904 was £2. It was clear to many educated, native Indians that the decline was contributed mainly by the continuous exploitation of India's resources by its British rulers.[5]

The price of gold had also fallen rapidly. While the rest of Europe purchased large quantities of gold from the United Kingdom, there was little increase in the financial reserves. This dealt a blow to an already deteriorating economy. The

United Kingdom began to look to its possessions such as India to compensate for the gold that was sold.

India was a primary supplier of raw materials during World War I. India provided large quantities of iron, steel and other raw material for the manufacture of arms and armaments. Industrialization and manufacturing production systems were slowly established. Indian cities were both suppliers as well as consuming markets for finished British goods.

When the First World War came to an end, concessions were made to Indians in return for their loyalty to the British Empire during the war. In 1923, the British Raj offered government protection to some industries, theoretically to industrialize the economy. However, these measures were only symbolic. In truth they were intended to finance and protect British enterprise since all the benefactors were British-run industries.

At the onset of the Great Depression, as it had been for decades, much of India's imports were from the United Kingdom.

During the Depression, the British Raj intensified the existing imperialistic economic policies. While these policies protected Britain's economy, they aided in destroying India's. Because the fall in prices had been higher in India compared to the rest of the world, the price of commodities manufactured in India rose dramatically compared to imports from the United Kingdom or some other countries in the world. Farmers who were cultivating food crops had earlier moved over to cash crop cultivation in large numbers to meet the demands of the mills in the United Kingdom. Now, they were crippled as they were unable to sell their products in India due to the high prices; nor could they export the commodities to the United Kingdom which had recently adopted a protective policy prohibiting imports from India.

Rice and wheat could be used for private consumption but the cash crops, such as cotton, which native Indians now cultivated could not be used for public consumption. As there was little or no sale of indigenous manufactured items and limited exports, commodities accumulated and the flow of cash was restricted. Moreover, imports were severely affected by the Swadeshi movement and the boycott of foreign goods imposed by Indian nationalists. There was a deficiency of money in many places causing widespread poverty and unrest in many households.

It was this backdrop of economic conditions that the middle class LeStyne's lived.

One Friday night, Dolly finished changing into her nightgown and quickly walked out of the bedroom.

The two looked at each other for but a second. They were both in love still, but tired. Their eyes darted away from each other.

She was afraid that looking straight at him would start another argument, as was the case many times this past few months. Their arguments were coming on more frequently, and with no real reason to them, she thought.

"James, remember we have to go to your sister's house tomorrow to help her pack," Dolly reminded James.

"I completely bloody forgot," said James, "Can you go with Ramesh (the servant man) for me?"

"No, I can not. Not again to another outing with Ramesh! Besides I'm going with the ladies from the association to Saturday tea," said Dolly. There was a stained pause.

"Maybe you can help your sister in the late afternoon," said Dolly softly. "She is your sister, and this move has become very traumatic for her...for all of us."

"Yes, but I really need to catch up with work. Too many things going on at work and Mr. Chapman needs me to be there this weekend," James said.

"You are planning on working again this weekend?" said Dolly growing angrier.

"I can not manage with the house projects, while you run away to work again," said Dolly.

"Well, we need for me to keep this job. Everyone is losing jobs," said James.

"Yes, but we deserve a private life and time for ourselves," said Dolly. "You need to learn to say No to that boss of yours."

"No, no, no," said James. "See I can say No." he joked, trying to lighten the mood.

"Yes, now can't you say it to your overbearing, manipulative boss," Dolly said.

At that, James' mood changed. "You think Chapman is manipulative and that I am but a pawn being manipulated?" James said growing angrier. "You think that I would let myself be foolish like that?"

"I think that you just don't really know how to say No," said Dolly.

A long pause saturated the room.

James walked to their bedroom and closed the door. He undressed in silence, and then sat on the settee near the window. This was his favorite spot when he wanted to concentrate and get his thoughts together.

"She doesn't understand," he said out loud to himself and slowly lowered his chin to his chest, hanging his head in frustration.

The consequences of worldwide urbanization and eventually the Depression had its impact on the middle class in British India. Previously, movement within the ranks was possible after 1 or 2 generations, but after the Depression it was almost impossible among the Anglo-Indians in India.

The problem was that those who worked to get higher in the ranks were subject to move to a position that might become obsolete or that they might fall victim to the ambitions of new British officers and civilians coming from England.

Although a good worker, In 1928 James lost his job, as did so many British and Anglo-Indians working in the Telegraph at that time. Fewer telegrams were being sent, while more telephones were being installed.

Although they had fallen on difficult times, Dolly and James so loved each other they could not help but want children. In late 1928 when Dolly learned of her pregnancy she was pleased, but concerned about how they would live.

Due to the threat of the Depression alone, they saw how their lives changed dramatically because they had barely enough to live on from month to month. Additional fear of what would happen with the baby on the way caused James and Dolly to confront the truth — they needed help.

When someone made a comment on the child's upcoming arrival, Dolly said "I can't believe that I'm having a baby!" It seemed absolutely frightening to her to be pregnant and that she was going to have to take care of a baby. All she wanted was to be with James still. She wanted the best environment for the baby, but knew she was going to need help. With the economic turmoil of the country she knew that it would be best with someone she can trust.

Since Dolly's mother's home was not an option, they thought about another place to live. Dolly and James packed up their belongings and moved in with his parents to save money and be close to loved ones. It was then that Florence DeQuadros-LeStyne and George LeStyne opened their doors and hearts to the new couple.

Yvonne LeStyne, was born in a small Catholic hospital in Bombay on July 3, 1929, just weeks before the start of the Depression. The hospital staff of nuns and English doctors looked after mother and child. When she was ready to take her home, Dolly brought Yvonne home to Santa Cruz, Bombay. Dolly, James, and Yvonne stayed with James' mother and father in Santa Cruz, Bombay for about a year until they moved to another home down the block from their in-laws.

Shortly after Yvonne's birth, in December 1929, a session of the Indian National Congress was held on the banks of the river Ravi in Lahore. Congress President Jawaharlal Nehru declared that complete independence from British rule would, henceforth, 'be the goal of the Congress". Till now, this was a change in thinking for the Indian National Congress. It was not anticipated by the British, but understood to be an eventuality and wished for in the hearts of many Indians. This announcement by Nehru triggered the Civil Disobedience Movement throughout India, which commenced with the Salt Satyagraha (Salt March).

Salt was needed to keep any type of food fresh in India. It was a necessity.

The Salt Satyagraha formed the highpoint of the Civil Disobedience Movement. While the heavy salt tax was always a burden to the poor Indian peasant, the widespread poverty during the Great Depression made it even more difficult for the common, low to middle class Indian or Anglo-Indian to procure salt. In response to this tax, between March 1930 and April 1930, Mahatma Gandhi marched with over 30,000 followers to the coastal town of Dandi in Gujarat, where they illegally manufactured salt. [6]

James and his father read the newspapers with sighs of disgust. "They have defied the Government," said George. "But it is a monopoly on salt father," said James. "Is it fair to have a monopoly on salt in this or any country? How could they permit it?"

Subsequently, similar marches were organized at Dharasana and Vedaranyam. The Government responded with a massive retaliation and arrests, of which Ghandi was among them, but by then, the media coverage of events had fundamentally molded international and Anglo-Indian opinion.

Contributing to the matter were issues with the existing caste system and how it affected the middle class in India. There was a caste system in India that Anglo-Indian families inadvertently adhered to. It was a part of their culture.

Under this caste system, which has origins within Hinduism, people were categorized by their occupations. Although originally caste depended upon a person's work, it soon became hereditary. Each person was born into an unalterable social status.

At the lowest stratum were the Untouchables. The Untouchables were hired to do work that members of the caste system would not do. These jobs included killing or disposing of dead cattle or working with their hides. The untouchables also worked as sweepers, washers, or in other jobs that required contact with human emissions such as sweat, urine, or feces.

The untouchables served many people, including the Indians, British, and Anglo-Indians.

They contributed to the stability of the middle-class Anglo-Indian way of life.

Gandhi's Quest

Dolly's Anglo-Indian family saw the little brown man move a nation.

In the meantime, western power was changing. Power resulted, not only from superiority in the military, but in the sciences and more. Possibly, its overwhelming claim to fame was Britain's ability to turn properties into nation-states. In all projects, it seemed Britain's corporations and military had humiliated the Indian natives and come to dominate India. It's clear that many native Indians were resentful of conquerors, but also envious. Radical groups were formed to discuss and deal with their resentment and envy—managing these two feelings were imperative tasks within the ranks of these groups.

At that time, possibly the most popular and radical figure in the eyes of the Anglo-Indian at the time was Mohandas K. Gandhi. Gandhi believed that western society was based on a voracious use of national resources that required the ongoing quest for new sources of raw materials and markets.

It was right before Yvonne was born that James heard the news of Gandhi's political and social activities and finally took note of the "Gandhi" name more seriously. Gandhi's thinking was that the economic imperialism of a single tiny island kingdom (England) was keeping the world in chains and profoundly exploiting the colonies it touched economically — stripping them bare like locusts.[7]

Dolly bonds with her In-Laws

The relationship between Dolly and her mother-in-law grew stronger and she knew she was someone she could trust to share her own feelings and life with. Florence LeStyne took on the task of tending to Yvonne with the nurse maid. Yvonne was the first, and therefore treated special. But as months grew into years, and more children followed, all could see that the oldest child of the brood inadvertently got most of the attention.

For Dolly, five boys followed one after another, about 2 years apart. All the boys were darker-skinned like their father except for Carlyle and Colin, who had light brown skin, blondish-brown hair and blue-eyes like their Grandfather Alfred. Dolly's growing family moved to Kirkee for a place they could call their own and bigger quarters.

James' parents, Florence and George followed them to Kirkee by 1934. George had a good pension—about 350 Rupees per month, so they were able to retire closer to their grandchildren. They managed to hire some new servants to help with the house and their activities, and spent their extra time helping Dolly and James with their babies.

The young Yvonne was adored by her Grandmother Florence. Yvonne called her grandmother Nana and they were, as many witnessed, inseparable. By the age of 3, Yvonne and Florence developed a tight relationship that both kept for more than a decade before she left for school. While Dolly and James managed with their 5 boys, Florence kept her grand-daughter, Yvonne close by her.

Florence LeStyne (nee DeQuadros), who had lived in Goa for years before coming to Bombay, was of Portuguese descent. Her mother was from Italy and her father was from Portugal. Her father, Sir Michael DeQuadros had reportedly been knighted by Queen Victoria. He was knighted for his charity/volunteer work that helped build the *Jesus and Mary Convent* in Bombay. His wife, Lady Anne DeQuadros and he enjoyed a comfortable life in Goa and then later went to various cities in southern and northern India.

Florence met and married George LeStyne at the age of 16. She proceeded to have 15 children, but only 5 lived.

Florence came from a well-respected Portuguese family in Goa, with her marriage providing George LeStyne with connections. Her marriage to George opened doors for him. He may have been a dark Anglo-Indian than the lighter-skinned British and other fair Anglo-Indians, but he still managed to obtain an important position within the telegraph, which he was always grateful for. His respect and jovial personality caused him to be well liked and move up steadily to a coveted position, and then later bring on his son.

By 1900 George was the superintendent of telephone and telegraph in Bombay and his house was filled with servants to clean, cook and take care of the children. Florence and George together became a well respected Anglo-Indian family, and were relatively well off with a large home, many servants, and lives where they never wanted for much.

But the Depression had a severe impact on Florence, George and the entire family. It was before and during the depression that George's son James and others in their family lost jobs and became unemployed.

Unemployment in India had hit the middle and lower middle classes the most harshly, and the Anglo-Indian community fit into those stratums. Unemployment among the Anglo-

Indians reached its peak about 1923.[8] In other places around the world it was 1929.

James was not so naïve to see that his father's influence had a bearing on his own position within the organization, but even his father, George could not help him. James saw things were getting worse. After years of passing through Chowringhee and being accosted by scores of starving Indian men and children, mostly in rags, showing all the dreadful effects of hunger with their fallen eyes and emaciated bodies, he started to see Anglo-Indians among the crowd. One night in fact, as he walked through the park closest to his workplace to go back to do more work he wanted to finish off, he was shocked to see on his way home at 11:00pm, groups of Europeans and Anglo-Indian women and children sleeping on the grass, with only the sky as their ceiling. He also saw a few by the stables sleeping with the animals.

This was a rare sight, as the Europeans and Anglo-Indians were the last to show the effects of the Depression and the first to recover. They were typically, if hurt financially, just likely to take cheaper living quarters.

Through the years he never told his daughter or sons about such things, but again and again, on quiet nights he would recount the horror to his wife. He swore he would do anything to avoid such an outcome for his family.

After months of being unemployed, James settled for a position within the army, but always felt cheated out of a better position. British, who were coming over to India because of the failing economy over there, he felt, robbed the positions from people like him. He longed for that better position and resented any Brits that got them.

Day after day, James told his wife how he tried to find work, but nothing suitable was available. When he did hear of a job, he learned that others or those who inquired about the job, which were many, had many letters of recommendation.

Within a few years the Depression became worse and no solid lead had turned up, but he held strong and always remembered that connections within the Anglo-Indian community were most important.

A global economic depression broke out in 1929 following the American stock market crash of 1929.

The causes were diverse, with the rise in costs and economic inflation of the post-war period being one of the main reasons. This inflation was caused by excessive manufacturing activities during the First World War throughout the European provinces, of which one was the Indian sub-continent. As a result, huge amounts of products were piled up without being used.

Wartime expenditure had reduced the countries of Europe to a state of heavy debt. Protective economic policies of European countries made their condition even worse—especially for India. The United States of America was not so heavily affected as India, partly because it had participated on the side of the victorious Allies and partly because the American mainland states were never really under attack during the span of the war, but only in the state of Hawaii (away from the mainland). As a result, the United States of America emerged as a financial superpower and the principal creditor to European countries.

The Treaty of Versailles and its conditions had subsequently impoverished Germany. Germany lost a lot due to its involvement in the war and owed extremely high debts. Germany paid off its debts by borrowing from the United Kingdom. The United Kingdom, meanwhile, paid Germany by borrowing from the United States of America. This created a situation wherein most European countries became dependant on the United States of America.

James and family heard of the U.S.'s ability to withstand the storm and admired it from afar. "Maybe it is not a country of just Hollywood stars, but something else is there," said Florence to her daughter-in-law.

When the American stock market suffered its crash in the Fall of 1929, it triggered several actions, of which one was to stop providing loans to foreign countries, thereby leading to a global financial disaster for England and in turn India, which had grown almost completely reliant on England.

It was finally in 1932, when an opportunity arose for James. James heard of the job from his Cousin Kathleen's husband. Reluctantly at first, but because of his wife's perseverance, Kathleen contacted a well-known Anglo Indian in the community called Sir Henry Gidney with a letter requesting an audience. Although with his management skills, they thought any letters of recommendation would help lock in the position.

The Anglo-Indian
Community's Grasp
for Support

Gidney was considered a competent leader on behalf of the Anglo-Indian community. He took up strong support on behalf of members of those especially in the Anglo-Indian community employed in the Posts and Telegraph Department, so of course he knew of James' and his father.

Gidney was drawn into public service when in 1918 he was elected president of the Bombay branch of the Anglo-Indian Empire League. He embraced the position and all its political suggestions. He ended up serving on several committees through the years to help toward specific Anglo-Indian causes. [9] Gidney didn't always get what he wanted for the Anglo-Indians in the railway or telegraph industries, but managed with his ability to organize and orchestrate positive publicity and in turn positive momentum for the organization.

He managed to have a memorandum drawn up with Lord Birkenhead, the secretary of state at the time, emphasizing the special difficulties of the Anglo-Indian community with regard to its political and legal position in the country, the threat to its employment in the services, and its economic and cultural well-being.

One feature of the memo, underlined Gidney's own difficult position. As a leader, Gidney was not able to have the community move ahead, and in actuality, just barely kept their position from deteriorating any further as a result of the Indian independence movement.

Among his political opponents was J.H. Abbott, who had been the President of the Empire League for many years. Abbott also represented the community in the then Imperial Legislative Council. The other was H.A. Stark, who achieved distinction as an educator within the community and wrote a number of historical pieces related to the community. But Stark did not have the engaging flair and leadership skills that Gidney had, and although Abbott did, Abbott was no match for Gidney's strong ability to challenge on a common platform, and incomparable greater capacity and polish.

As a result of the decisive support of the community throughout the country for Gidney, Gidney was nominated by the Viceroy to the Legislative Assembly and took his seat in the House in September 1921.

There were five organizations representing Anglo-Indians in different parts of the country including Gidney's league. In April 1926, there was a conference between the representatives of these organizations from Bombay, Bengal, Madras, Allahabad, and Burma. The goal was amalgamation. Everyone appeared initially to have their own agenda, but the Bengal and Burma leaned toward amalgamation and unity. Gidney subsequently became president of the Bengal Organization. Into this he fused his own Bombay-based organization. The Anglo Indian and Domiciled European Association, the All India group and Burma were finally unified.

By 1929, Allahabad also came under Gidney's banner organization and more respect and notoriety followed. He was able to organize the entire Anglo-Indian community throughout India under one umbrella and become its spokesperson.

Still, because of his pride, James went reluctantly to Gidney. Because of his wife and cousin's insistence, and a possible opportunity in Depression-era India he went and declared to Gidney that there is a fine job in the Armory available and that he is very interested in it, then asked if Gidney could write a letter of referral for him.

They spoke for some time and then he agreed, "Sir, I am very comfortable giving this referral. Give me the pertinent details and I'll make sure to highlight your best qualities."

He wrote a convincing letter, even without knowing his direct professional and academic record, but only of his work ethics. Referrals from friends who do not know the applicant in a business relationship did not typically carry much weight, but the officers within the Armory knew of Gidney and his position and James was hired without delay.

Keeping the Family Together

After James held that armory position for a certain amount of time, he came back home one day and said to his family that "we are all moving, because the job at the Arsenal is closer to Kirkee," Poona and Kirkee were located adjacent to each other.

The British had been in the Poona region since the 1820s. They had put Poona under the Bombay Presidency. The City became central to the development of ammunition and firearms, thus the Armory's importance. During their reign, the British set up an extensive ammunition factory there and this still exists till today and is now used by the Indian Army.

By 1934, James had saved enough and before they knew it the family was off to Kirkee. Later, after James and Dolly settled in Kirkee, other relatives followed: Millie Heaton's family, Kathleen Stevens family, George and Florence, and others. They all came to Kirkee or Poona and ended up living next door to each other.

Because the Anglo-Indians were somewhat transient in nature, most did not buy land, but instead rented. The family—George and Florence, James and Dolly, Millie Heaton, Berle Stratham all rented and never thought otherwise—to buy land in India. Many Parsis and Indians primarily owned the land where they lived and paid a tax to the British.

The family preferred to concentrate on living in a comfortable way close to each other, rather than buy property that was far and separate from family and the Anglo-Indian community that they had grown comfortable with. Although a good business deal that they could afford with money pooled together, it was during (and afterwards) the Depression and they preferred not to take the risk.

Yvonne's Aunt Millie Heaton lived on one side, and her mother lived on the other side. Yvonne's grandmother Florence and grandfather George joined in a house with an open air flat across the courtyard. All the houses were on the same street.

With Florence next door, the bond between grandmother and grandchild had no where to go, but to get stronger. Yvonne slept, woke, clothed, and ate breakfast, lunch and dinner in her grandmother's house. She rarely went to her mother's house although she lived close by. She just stayed with her Grandmother. "I could go visit Mum and Daddy at any time Nana. I'll stay here," Yvonne would say to her Grandmother.

But, her mother Dolly had other kids to tend to. By this time the novelty of baby-rearing had decreased considerably for Dolly. The children demanded so much attention and grew so attached to her heart. She always felt a need to please them trying to find ways to comfort them. The children were curious, unpredictable, and moody. Even with help from servants, it was harder work than she ever imagined.

She had all her boys under one roof. There was a tendency in the Anglo-Indian community to adopt names with an Anglo-Saxon facade. Yvonne's brothers George, Colin, Carlyle (Carl), Reginald (Reggie), and Gerald (Gerry) all had Anglo-Saxon names. The boys saw their father without a job and struggling. The impact of the times on the family was devastating. Many people lost their homes and were forced to live in paltry dwellings in Shanty towns. Being an unemployed Anglo-Indian was seen as very shameful and degrading.

Even in the wake of the Great Depression, James managed to get that job at the Arsenal, yet he always felt the job was beneath him, beneath the job that he originally had at the Telegraph. In the meantime, Dolly tended to her 5 "difficult" boys, as she would often call them. "Good for Nothing, Paria

Dogs", she would lightheartedly complain. "Wait till your Father comes home. You will hear from him then," she often warned them.

But, when poor James did come home, he did not know how to deal with it at all. As years passed, stories abounded within the family and amongst neighbors about how the boys were always in some trouble or another. The parents did not outwardly show their warm and loving inclinations, but were more reserved and conservative. Dolly, especially was very conservative and rarely laughed and played with her kids. Playing with the kids was not a normal activity for an English-bred mother as she was.

The boys played in the streets and had pranks running on neighbors and friends. They stopped to go to watering holes when it was sweltering hot and skipped school on days they saw an opportunity for fun.

James would let things go sometimes, but ended up punishing the boys for harming his and their mother's reputation within the community—An Anglo-Indian community where reputation was everything. Through the seasons, the boys tried to pretend that the beatings were coming to an end. Eventually, the boys stood proud and strong and moved on, because that is the Anglo-Indian way.

However, eventually two of them grew no longer strong, nor could move forward. When they grew older and had difficulty adjusting, they fell into gambling and drinking. They eventually said sorry to their own families and in the end lost the fight to cope and took their own lives.

In their minds, they might have felt unforgiven, but if they only understood early on that it wasn't their fault.

High Tea and Talk
of Anglo India

Children are singing in the distance..."*God save our gracious Queen, Live long our noble Queen, God save the Queen! Send her victorious, Happy and glorious, Long to reign over us, God save the Queen. Thy choicest gifts in store On her be pleased to pour, Long may she reign; May she defend our laws, And ever give us cause to sing with heart and voice, God save the Queen! God bless our native land, May heaven's protective hand Still guard our shore; May peace her power extend, Foe be transformed to friend, And Britain's power depend On war no more. May just and righteous laws uphold the public cause, And bless our isle. Home of the brave and free, Fair land and liberty, We pray that still on thee Kind heaven may smile. And not this land alone- But be thy mercies known From shore to shore. Lord, make the nations see That men should brothers be, and from one family the wide world o'er...*

Florence had been out traveling with her servant-man, again to her little street in Kirkee known as Elephantstone Road listening to the school children sing in the distance. She enjoyed the opportunity to travel as she wished, without her husband sometimes, but knew it was getting too risky to do so in these unpredictable times with protests and marches.

She watched the house numbers and stopped in front of her son's home, not far from her own. His was a warm, bright peach bungalow, the kind so popular amongst Anglo-Indians in the 1920s and 1930s. When she rang the bell, Sasha, the Indian servant girl answered the door immediately.

Florence greeted her with a nod and made her way around the veranda into the large family room. There were 3 bedrooms and 2 bathrooms on the other side of the house.

Dolly and James had one bedroom, while the kids were in the other. A nurse maid was called upon to help with the infants.

Florence called out to her favorite granddaughter Yvonne. "Yvonne, I'm on the Veranda. When you are ready come down." Trellis work covered the front patio and Florence loved it so, reminding her of days gone by with her father and mother in wealthier times.

Four-year old Yvonne was on the back of the veranda playing with her nanny, who had been one of the servant girls in prior years.

"Grandma," screamed little Yvonne. "You are here!" she said with a widening smile.

"Yvonne," she smiled back to her beloved grandchild and the nanny, Laxmi who was standing next to her. "Where is your mother?" Florence bent down to ask little Yvonne.

"K-chicken Grandma," said Yvonne smiling.

When Florence arrived, Dolly was talking with her friend Kitty Silver in the Kitchen. She stood by the wall and listened to Dolly talk with her friend.

Dolly's friends were all Anglo-Indian and Florence could hear them chattering away about doctors in the area. "Pregnant again. I will need to find a doctor that lives closer..." and the words trailed off.

"Kitty, I would like to introduce you to my mother-in-law, Florence LeStyne."

"Mrs. LeStyne, How are you? Kitty said to Florence with her hand extended. "We have met on more than one occasion," Kitty said to Dolly.

"Yes, Kitty, it is so wonderful to see you again," Florence said.

There was a tendency in the Anglo-Indian community to adopt first names with an Anglo-Saxon ring, but people changed their surnames and sometimes first names to be seen as even more British. As was the case with D'Silva; It was changed to Silver, and Ferenandez to Ferns. They did it more because it was acceptable in the community and less because it would draw criticism if done otherwise.

Some people in the Anglo-Indian community had Goan names, but they really had little to do with Goa. In Yvonne's case her ancestors did come from Goa, but did not have Goan names.

"Sit down Mrs. LeStyne. We were just having Afternoon Tea. Would you like some?"

"Yes, thank you." smiled Florence. "You can call me Florence."

"I was just going to ask Sasha to bring me some Chapattis and Parathas with curry. I'm starved," said Florence to the cook.

The servant girl, nodded her head and said, "Maam, we have prepared High Tea. It will be ready shortly,"

"Ok, that's fine," said Dolly. "Mother, would you like some Chapattis on the side with the tea?"

"Yes, Dolly," said Florence. Dolly asked the cook to prepare that as well for her mother in-law.

Although she enjoyed the Royal British black tea, Florence had grown accustomed by now to Ceylon tea. This was tea Florence drank among her Anglo-Indian friends and so it became a staple for her daughter and their friends.

The Colombo Tea Traders' Association and the Tea Research Institute helped export Ceylon Teas out of India and boost the demand through marketing throughout India and the world, making it a regular in tea houses in England and among Anglo-Indian households.

Finger sandwiches, scones and some Indian sweetmeats were served with the tea.

"Mother, how are you? Have you come from the market, or did you just stop by to see Yvonne?" said Dolly.

"To see you and Yvonne and the babies of course," said Florence.

They sat and had small talk before Kitty asked a question quite out of the blue.

"Dolly, what is your family's background?" Kitty asked.

"My Goodness. Well, there is some Indian blood in us, but I don't know of the details because we never spoke about it," said Dolly.

"It's a result of the Indians mixing with the English," said Florence pushing into the conversation "generation after generation born in India. ...so we are Anglo-Indians now. "

"I am actually of Portuguese descent, from Goa," said Florence to Kitty. "I was born in Bombay, but George's and my family histories are from Goa."

"They were Portuguese according to our family tree with some Italian," said Florence.

"So we have Italian blood and Portuguese blood on my father's side," said Florence. "The Family names were De Quadros and De Lima."

"Most people in Goa are mixed with Portuguese. Maybe that's where the darker skin comes from," said Florence.

"Is that why Yvonne is so light and her cousins so dark?" asked Kitty.

Dolly's mother-in-law Florence thought for a moment.

Dolly had been introduced to James' siblings at family gatherings and parties, but seldom heard her mother-in-law talk about the family. One of her favorite sister-in-laws was Millie, who she loved dearly and whose son Cecil was about the same age as Yvonne. She had already met James' sisters Birdie, Beryl, and Vivian and felt a part of the family with all of them.

Beryl and her husband constantly went to the club in Santa Cruz to play cards and chat with friends, so Dolly rarely met with her as she was always busy doing something with her children.

"Well, that's not where our youngest Carlyle's blond hair, gray eyes and fair skin comes from," Dolly smiled.

"And, well the other little one is ½ light and ½ dark," said Dolly.

"Have you met the boys?" Florence asked Kitty.

"Yes, all except Colin," said Kitty.

"He is always crawling around causing mischief somewhere in the house," said Dolly.

"I married James, which was a taboo among my *English* family." said Dolly. "My mother was so English and to her, marrying a darker Anglo-Indian, well, that was against the English way. People were very prejudiced."

"They still are...," said Kitty.

"True friends won't care," said Florence smiling and waving her hands in the air. "Who needs the damn mutlaby (fair weather friends)?"

"Kitty, what typically helped determine the attitude toward Dolly's marriage and acceptance of her and James was my husband's good status in this community. If it weren't for his position within the Telegraph organization, where would we all be?" declared Florence.

"Yes, mother," Dolly said turning to Kitty and smiling. "Where would we all be?" She put back hand across her head as though fainting.

Dolly laughed as she had heard it all more than once before from her father-in-law and husband— the proud stories and history of the telegraph in that country. It was about 1851 when the first electric telegraph line was started between Calcutta (which was the capital at the time) and Diamond Harbour (near the Bay of Bengal) by the British East India Company. The Posts and Telegraphs department, which was a part of the Public Works Department, was given an increased budget and took on more and more projects. Soon, it had built 6,000 km of telegraph lines connecting major centers such as Calcutta, Bombay and Madras with other centers in the North, as well as Bangalore in the South. At that point in 1854, a separate department was created called the Post and Telegraph dept. Telegraph facilities eventually were opened to the public and began to be used everyday. It transitioned from being a luxury to a public utility.

The Oriental Telephone Company was established on January 25, 1881, as the result of an agreement between Thomas Edison, Alexander Graham Bell, the Oriental Bell Telephone Company of New York and the Anglo-Indian Telephone Company, Ltd.[10]

In 1891, the British run Government in India issued a license to the Oriental Telephone Company Ltd of England to open telephone exchanges in Calcutta, Bombay, Madras and Ahmadabad. This became the first formal telephone service established in India.

Initially the British government refused permission to build the company on the grounds that the establishment of a communications network, involving telephones, was a Government interest. The British government itself wanted to undertake the work. After much thought though, they saw that if it were Anglo-Indians running it they were going to be in charge anyway. Thus was the start of the Indian Telephone and Telegraph office where Dolly's father-in-law worked.

"You kids take these luxuries like telephones for granted. With the way things are going –my goodness I am quite scared of it all with War threatening and all," said Florence. "Thank goodness you had a proper education. But this one…" and she picked up Yvonne onto her lap. "She will have the best education and be brought up as a proper lady."

Acceptance was key for a comfortable life within the Anglo-Indian community. Most of Dolly and her Mother-In

Law's friends were Anglo-Indian. There was a certain social behavior in the community in the sense that many of its social functions were confined to members of only the community. This was a reflection of the social pattern and stratum there in India to keep everything among this group.

It is not, that they were unsociable. They were sociable, but feared being looked down upon considerably if mingling with the wrong crowd.

There was a certain camaraderie within the community (club), but not so much outside of "the club".

The club was a social space that figured prominently in colonial British India, a place where British officials and the very rich shared exaggerated stories of adventure and romance. During the 20th century it was a quiet, after-work refuge for men, where they could sit and drink whiskey, gossip, read the latest newspaper and retain the community's illusion of stability.

Entry into these clubs was based on social status. There were clubs for officers, clubs for enlisted men, clubs for Eurasians, and then there were clubs where only Anglo-Indians met.

"Oh mother, who is an Anglo-Indian anyway?" asked Dolly as little Yvonne listened in.

Dolly thought about her biological mother—Evelyn. She was forever "British" in her eyes.

"Well, it's everyone," said Florence.

"…and no one," said Kitty.

Dolly laughed and showed her wide eyes and large front teeth. "You are so funny Kitty."

Kitty Silver, or K West as her friends nicknamed her, was from Calcutta like Dolly—the girls attended school together. Kitty became friendly with Dolly's brother Jack, but he ended up marrying Irene (Ivy), a born and bred English woman. Of course, with Kitty being Anglo-Indian, she was not as acceptable for a match with Jack as Ivy.

"Yes, well surely, the community has, in fact, traversed several name changes," said Florence."Anglo-Indian—it is kindly used by British fathers about their Indian-born sons at one time. We used to say Indo-Briton, then Eurasians, and even East Indians, but some of these terms seemed to take on a derogatory tone. But Anglo-Indian has stuck for a long time within the community. Hasn't it now?"

Kitty suddenly stood up tall, and gave a mock military salute. Then with a hardy smile and her head held high, she mimicked the founder of the first Imperial Anglo-Indian Association, the late Dr. Wallace, who she had met at a dinner at one time with her mother. "Regardless, Britishers we are, and Britishers we ever must be," Kitty exclaimed.

Both Dolly and Kitty laughed out loud. Florence looked at them like she thought they were crazy.

"Seriously though, as I understand, we are officially recognized by the government as Anglo-Indian and should use of the term *Anglo-Indian*," said Kitty. "The term was used to describe Britons working or residing in India. It was refused though, because of Dr. Wallace —his thinking was "Once we accept this name and permit ourselves to be styled Eurasian or statutory natives of India we become estranged from our proud heritage of Britishers."

"You know," said Florence, "Anglo-Indian used to mean any European inhabitant of colonial India. But what of Kipling, who was a country-born Britisher, born in Bombay?" she said referring to Rudyard Kipling the well-respected author.

"I don't know, but we have our own mannerisms and customs here, different from what England has. You can clearly see who is a Brit and who is an Anglo-Indian," said Dolly.

"Yes, I guess we are in an Identity crisis of our own," Kitty smiled. "We are British, but Indian as well."

"Florence do you know that I went to school with a very famous Anglo-Indian girl called Merle Oberon. We called her Queenie. Queenie O'Brien," said Dolly to her Mother-In-Law.

"No, you didn't! Yes. I have certainly heard of Queenie O-Brien," said Florence.

"Yes. Kitty I think that you might have known her mother. Merle went around with Charlotte, her mother, as her servant because her mother was so dark. She didn't want to let people know it was her mother."

"Is that true?" asked Kitty.

These movie stars are so shallow," said Florence.

"Well maybe, but you must know the whole story. I don't believe it bothered her mother as much as you think. I think she really was happy to have her daughter get that far in the entertainment industry.

"I went to private school with Merle when I lived with my Mum in Calcutta," said Dolly. "Charlotte, who was my mother's age, studied in India and became a nurses' assistant. She was very capable. She tended to go around with a few men I hear. She eventually met this Irish engineer, who was commissioned on the railways, named Arthur. You know all these Anglo-Indian men were working the railways and Arthur O' Brien was no different. Anyway, Charlotte soon found herself pregnant and Arthur and Charlotte married. I believe he did love her very much. Then in about 1910, he found out that he was being transferred to the Victoria Station in Bombay to work on the railway there. You know with the war going on, so much traveling and so many cargo shipments taking place there was plenty of work--not like today. Eventually, Charlotte and he left for Bombay during the war. Hospitals were dealing with an abundance of patients and far too little staff, so of course Charlotte was easily able to find a full nursing job there," said Dolly.

"When did Charlotte have Merle?" asked Kitty.

"By 1911, little Merle, with her hazel eyes and that creamy light complexion was born. Merle, aka, Queenie as we called her, was taken in by everyone. Her true name was Estelle Merle O'Brien Thompson. She just had that way about her

—Very sweet and outgoing and her laugh. Oh my Lord…so infectious."

"Why is she named Queenie," asked Kitty.

"Queenie O'Brien…if you believe that," said Dolly.

"It had something to do with Queen Mary coming. King George V and Queen Mary came to Bombay the year she was born and I think she was playfully nicknamed Queenie and it stuck. As she got older she really became more beautiful, with those green eyes," said Dolly.

"Mother, what year did the war break out?" asked Dolly.

"I think it was 1914 honey, between Germany and England," said Florence.

"Oh yes, 1914, and so Arthur, Merle's father—feeling he was still young and strong enough, enlisted to fight for England. Well, to everyone's shock he died."

"From what? A bullet to the head during a battle?" asked Florence.

"No! But that's what I thought. I think he became sick and just never recovered," said Dolly.

"Charlotte and Merle were devastated, but they picked themselves up and eventually moved into the Imperial Mansion in Bombay."

"You mean that beautiful old building on Riphon road?" asked Kitty riveted by the story.

"Yes. I just took Yvonne near there the other day. There's a garden park right there. Anyway, I believe it was there in the Imperial Mansion that Merle really started feeling that she was an Anglo-Indian. She began to experience life from being from two different bloodlines—English and Indian, instead of that "pure English" background, said Dolly.

Merle had a half sister named Constance too. She was sent to the Taylor School in Poona. After she graduated she met this boy Alexander from Goa," said Dolly.

"Was he English?" asked Florence.

"No, she probably would have preferred an Englishman, but Alexander was Anglo-Indian like us and he had money and a relatively important position in society. I don't know much more about him."

"As I understand, Merle and her mother were not at her sister's wedding," said Dolly. "They may have been busy with other things."

"Regardless, that brings us to how we met," said Dolly.

"Finally," teased Kitty.

"Don't be so insolent," Dolly smiled at her friend.

"At any rate, before you knew it, Charlotte and Merle packed their bags, furniture and clothes and took off to Calcutta. Well you know how Calcutta was in the early 20's –full of life, and more ostentatious than today. English and Anglo-Indians adhered to the caste system…" said Dolly.

"… and believed that the white race was superior" said Kitty.

"Yes," agreed Dolly.

"Anyway, it was in Calcutta that Merle's mother enrolled her into La Martinere, where I also attended. It is a very prestigious girl's school. I went there for a few years, but had to leave," Dolly said with disappointment filling her face. My father had died and we just couldn't afford it."

"That's too bad Dolly," said Kitty. "Dolly, what was she like? What was Queenie really like?"

"My goodness, she always talked about films and the plots, and what she thought about this one playing this part in the film or that part in the film. She was popular and…beautiful. Very beautiful eyes," said Dolly.

"She didn't talk about wanting to be in the films?" asked Kitty.

"I don't remember that. I never really heard her say "I want to be a Hollywood star", said Dolly. She paused for second and then cleaned up around the table.

"But there were times, now that I look back, that she made me feel uncomfortable," said Dolly

"Why?" asked Kitty.

"Her mother Charlotte occasionally picked her up from the school. Well, she was so embarrassed when her mother would pick her up. It was probably partly a teenager reacting badly and partly embarrassment over how dark her mother was. Her mum was definitely darker than some of the servants, and always dressed in black. It was odd, but I think if Merle didn't feel uncomfortable we would have not felt so uncomfortable or thought so ill of the woman," Dolly explained.

"As she got older these rumors spread about her that she was actually an illegitimate child and that Arthur had abandoned her at birth—which is all not true."

"I think Merle was really too smart... and preoccupied for all that talk. She just kept on going, dreaming, planning."

"I lost touch with her. I heard from friends that Merle started going to dances, as we all did, but in Calcutta many of those girls were invited to clubs. And older men were there buying drinks, although it was prohibition. She ended up getting introduced to older men at these clubs. This is when Merle met Mark Hanna, the head of Paramount Pictures. He was the one who got her into wanting to be in films. Hanna eventually introduced her to an actor called Benjamin Finney and it was Merle and Ben that hit it off very well. They started out as good friends going everywhere together. Very much the gentleman. He treated her very well and you know probably would have married her, but then something happened. I don't know what, some speculate that it was that he met Charlotte one night and he was surprised to find out that she was not her servant, but her mother."

"Ben and Queenie are still friends I hear. My friend tells me that she doesn't think that relationship will go anywhere though. Ben had introduced Queenie to his friend Rex Ingram, who was a film director. He thought she looked very exotic and so he placed her as an extra in one of his films. After that, I heard she got small parts in films in France then England, and of course her mother goes everywhere with her. My friends say that she is like an actress herself…acting like a servant to Queenie," said Dolly.

Kitty chimed in and said, "Yes, she's in that new comedy *The Private Life of Henry VII*. I think she is playing a small part, but still it is Anne Boleyn," said Kitty to Florence.

"You are joking?—An Anglo-Indian playing Anne Boleyn, a Queen of England…Perfect," said Florence laughing.

All the women laughed loudly and long, and then they took another sip of tea.

"Anyway, knowing Merle, she will give it her all and make everyone remember her," said Dolly.

"Sounds like she may," Kitty said smiling.

Yvonne looked up smiling as all the women laughed and smiled. She smiled back and giggled.

An Outing with Grandparents

When Yvonne was five years old, her parents, Dolly and James moved to Poona, while Yvonne stayed on in Kirkee with her Grandmother and Grandfather Florence and George LeStyne.

At the beginning of each month, Yvonne's Grandpa was paid his check as superintendent of Telegraph, but he needed to go to Poona to pick it up. A horse and buggy driver was called and typically Yvonne, her brother Gerald and her cousin Cecil sat in the back and Florence and George sat in the front. Young Cecil, who was one year younger than Yvonne, begged to sit in the front seat next to the Tonga man so he could learn how to drive and of course Florence always indulged him.

"I want to sit in between Nana and Papa," said Yvonne, as she picked up her frilly silk dress and tried to move closer to them,"

"Yvonne, sit where you are. Take care of little Gerry," said James.

"Okay, but going home can I sit with you?" asked Yvonne.

"Yes, Yvonne that's fine," said Florence.

The road from Kirkee to Poona was filled with sounds and smells Yvonne would remember for a lifetime.

Although a short 10 miles away, the group grew quiet eventually and sat back enjoying the countryside, with farm animals, grass, and small homes speckling the landscape. Yvonne loved the Tonga ride with her cousin Cecil and her brother Gerald. They laughed so and loved to jump up every time they hit a bump in the road to make it feel more dramatic.

They arrived by early afternoon at the Bank of India to get "grandpa's pension check".

The Bank of India traces its roots through the Imperial Bank of India, and then even further back to the Bank of Calcutta, which made it the oldest Indian commercial bank.

Once the check was in hand, the children and grandparents went out for a special lunch.

They never encountered any problem in finding a place to eat. Poona had several restaurants, which offered cuisine ranging from Southern and Northern Indian, to English and Chinese. Florence preferred a full five-course meal, complete with the proper ambience and candle lights. Meanwhile the kids just wanted to find a place with pakoras and mango juice and then go shopping. Regardless, the food never disappointed Nana or Papa and the children.

Each time they passed restaurants along Fergusson College Road, a pub on Main Street, and the very fancy Shravan restaurant on Shivaji Nagar. But most impressive was the very British, Royal Restaurant on Eastern.

Many times the family agreed on the very fancy Kannalia Restaurant in Poona. The rest of the day was orchestrated by Grandmother shopping for clothing, food, liquor, and Indian Sweets. Yvonne's grandfather came along, patiently nodding, smiling, watching and listening, while helping to herd the children here and there.

In the early 1930s, the most common languages, spoken by a majority of the population in Poona were English and Marathi. A number of other Indian languages were also spoken in this small but growing suburban city. Marathi was then the official language of state of Maharashtra, where Poona is located. Apart from Marathi, Hindi was also one of the Indian languages used commonly throughout Poona.

Yvonne's Grandmother and Grandfather from Goa could both speak Hindustani and were able to get around and get things done, but they did not speak without some effort. Florence always had to struggle for a word here and there.

After the shopping, the family gathered for High Tea at 4:00pm at Dolly and James' house.

Bullock Carts and Glab Jamuns

The year is now 1938, and Yvonne is 9 years old. She and her family are still living in Kirkee. There were many ways in which they got around in India. Dolly's family covered long distances either walking on foot or using horse-drawn carriages. They would sometimes pass Indians who used bullock carts for transport, especially in and around Kirkee India and in rural areas. Typically, Dolly's servants would travel by or use the bullock cart to haul large items. Yvonne and one of her brothers had secretly sneaked a ride one sunny day with one the servants for a fun time.

The earlier arrival of the British brought change to India. Native Indians saw significant improvements in the horse carriages which were used for personal transport since early days. Dolly and her family would often call these carts tongas or buggies.

One hot, sunny day Yvonne and her mother Dolly left the market and headed home up Kusgav Hill.

The wheels of the Tonga turned slowly up the bumpy road. Chich, chich chi chch, ch.

They rode in silence toward their home.

"Mum, did you get Glab Jamuns?" asked Yvonne.

"No. I didn't buy Glab Jamuns," said Dolly.

"Why?" asked Yvonne.

"They are pure sugar balls honey," said Dolly.

"I am in love with them. I can eat 5 at one sitting," said Yvonne.

"Yes. I know that sweetheart, that's why I didn't get them," said Dolly.

"Ahhh Mum! Don't you like the Glab Jamuns?" asked Yvonne.

"Yes, but sometimes we need to buy the essentials: Meat and bread," said Dolly.

"If I was as rich as King George I would buy Glab Jamuns every day," Yvonne said.

Dolly smiled and then they both sat in silence.

"I feel like royalty mommy," said Yvonne.

"How so?" said Dolly.

"Because we are being carried by a bull."

Dolly laughed. "Yes, well you know you are related to royalty."

"Really. How?"

"Your Great grandfather—Nana Florence's father, Michael DeQuadros who grew up in Bombay, was knighted by Queen Elizabeth to become Sir Michael DeQuadros. His wife was Lady Ann DeQuadros.

"What did he do as a knight?" asked Yvonne.

"Nothing really honey, it's just a title, like an award for doing something special.

"What did he do that was special?" asked Yvonne

"He was acknowledged for all his charity work," said Dolly.

"That was nice of him Mum," said Yvonne.

"Yes, it was", and she looked down and smiled.

"Sir Michael DeQuadros was considered an important nobleman within the British and Anglo-Indian communities when he met Anne D'Lima (*Florence's Mother*). He courted her and took her for his wife as one day a man will court you and ask you to marry."

"I want to marry and have lots of kids Mum," said Yvonne.

"You do? Do you like taking care of children?" said Dolly.

"Yes. I love them," said Yvonne.

"Then maybe you should think about becoming a school teacher or children's nurse to be able to take care of them," said Dolly.

Yvonne looked at her mother and then looked out at the Indian landscape.

"I don't know. I will have to think about how to do that," thought Yvonne to herself.

The landscape unfolded into the string of Anglo-Indian bungalows on Elephantstone Road.

The Tonga came to a stop at the first Bungalow and both got out.

Family Ties

"Yvonne, Dolly you are back. You just missed Tilda," said Florence. Tilda was Florence's sister and Tilda's daughter was Kathleen Stevens, or as most of the kids in the family called her —Auntie Kathleen.

"Oh bugger. Was Kathleen with her? Well why didn't anyone tell me they were coming?" asked Dolly.

"Dolly, I will have all of the relatives over and we will have Tea one day soon," Florence tried to console Dolly. "No worries."

"But, you may not need to wait for that because I have news."

"What?" asked Yvonne.

"The news is that Auntie Kathleen and Uncle Paddy are coming to Kirkee to live," said Florence.

"Oh my. Fantastic," Dolly said.

"They found a place very close to us," said Florence.

Dolly sat down and requested the servants to put away all the food away in the pantry.

"I was just telling Yvonne about your mother Anne and your father Michael," Dolly said to Florence.

"Yes, Anne and Michael DeQuadros had 5 children: me— (pointing to herself), my sisters Tilda, Helen, and Juanita, and my brother Thomas," Florence said to Yvonne.

Juanita was living in Bombay--Calaba Causeway, then moved to Santa Cruz. I'm not sure what's happening with Thomas. Helen, poor thing, whispering to Dolly, died in a mental hospital in the early 1900s, and Tilda married a man named Dyson.

"I was the youngest out of the five," said Florence.

"Nana, when were you born?" asked Yvonne

"I was born in February of 1880 in Bombay. When I met George, we married almost instantly and starting trying to have kids," said Florence.

"As I understand, George was born April 1864 in Calicut and raised there," said Dolly.

Calcutta was a major city in the state of Kerala in southern India. Then, it was once known as the City of Spices for its role as a major port trading point of Eastern Spices. Merchants came from all over the world to sell their goods there.

Florence continued, "When my husband George was about 19 or 20 he changed his name by Deed poll from *George Alexander D'Silva* to George Alexander LeStyne, because LeStyne was his grandmother's surname," said Florence. "and he wanted to have a more British sounding name."

"So that is why some of the family is D'Silva and some are LeStyne?" asked Dolly.

"Yes," said Florence.

Dolly remembered that Florence had lost many children during childbirth and afterward.

"I remember you told me that you lost a number of children when they were just babies. So sorry about that Mum. It must have been a very hard thing."

"Oh Dolly, I was pregnant for many years. George and I had 15 children in all: 10 girls and 5 boys. But, ten died in childhood of sickness, stillborn, or disease—God Bless their souls. Only the 4 girls and my boy survived," she said with tears in her eyes.

"They are: Marie Florence, you know her as Birdie, and she was born in November of 1898; your husband George James was born in March 1903 (and as you know we all call him James), Vivienne Beatrice, born in September of 1905;

Millicent Teresa, who is Yvonne's Auntie Millie, was born in July of 1910, and Beryl Elizabeth, born in November of 1914."

"My goodness how I bet James was spoiled by his sisters," said Dolly.

"Oh yes, your James was revered by his sisters," said Florence.

"So, as the only boy he is expected to uphold the family name, with honor and respect," said Florence, putting her chin up defiantly.

Yvonne interrupted at that point, "Nana?"

"Yes, honey?"

"Is Auntie Kathleen coming with cousin Ivor and David?" asked Yvonne.

"Of course honey," said Florence.

"Oh Mommy," Yvonne turned to Dolly and whispered. "It will be such fun. David and Ivor will be able to play with us everyday," said Yvonne.

Green Chutney Heaven

Florence never cooked, but rather had her daughter Millie, or the servants cook and prepare the meals for her and her family and sometimes even Dolly's family.

Auntie Kathleen and Dolly would rarely walk into the kitchen to prepare a meal. Auntie Millie though, wanted dearly to cook and tried to at any chance she could. But together they talked and fussed about English and Irish meals, as well as spicy Indian curry recipes.

The majority of Anglo-Indians had retained diets rooted in Indian cuisine. The type of Indian cuisine a family favored was largely dependent on the region of India from which they were born in or the community from which it could trace its roots.

In Dolly's and Florence's houses Indian food was prepared with a variety of spices, including cumin, turmeric, chili powder, ginger, and garlic. Anglo-Indians ate a variety of dals (lentils) too, as well as beans and rice dishes. They also ate chicken, beef and pork.

Tandoori Chicken, a clay oven-baked chicken marinated in yogurt and spices, was a popular North Indian dish, as was Tandoori Fish. Biryani, flavored rice with vegetables and meat tossed in, was served on festive occasions, often accompanied by a cooling yogurt sauce called raita (rye-tah). Southern Indian dishes like masala, dosai (crepes filled with spiced potatoes) or idlis (idlees), and steamed rice cakes were also popular. Green chutneys made with mint or coriander accompanied a variety of savory fritters like the triangular, stuffed samosas. Pickled vegetables and fruits like lemons or mangoes were popular accompaniments to meals. A variety of unleavened breads like naans, rotis, and parathas were also eaten. Finally, "sweetmeats" like halva and burfi were often eaten by the family after a special meal.

Traditional Indian cooking tended to be a time-consuming process, so Anglo-Indians like Dolly, Auntie Kathleen, and Florence typically had servants to prepare their meals. Over the years, recipes were combined. As the modern food industry advanced with things like the electrical oven and the canning process, women found shortcuts such as canned or packaged/prepared parts of the meal using canned items or prepared parts of the meal to save time and effort.

Indian Patties were among their favorite.

Indian Patties (Anglo-Indian food served mostly at parties)

Meat Filling

> 500g minced beef
> 1 onion
> 2 cloves garlic
> Chili powder to taste
> 1 tspn ground Tumeric
> 1 tspn ground Corriander
> 2 tspns fresh Ginger
> 50 ml chopped mint
> Juice of 1 lemon
> 2 tblspns vegetable oil
> Salt, pepper to taste

Heat the oil in a frying pan, add the onion and garlic mix in the spices and seasoning and fry until all is soft. Add the minced beef, stirring until cooked. Remove from heat and stir in the mint and lemon juice.

Pastry

225gm. plain flour (1 cup)

2 tspns salt

2 tblsps vegetable oil (1/8 cup)

80 ml warm water (1/3 cup)

Mix flour and salt into a bowl. Make a well into the center and add the oil and enough water to make a firm dough. Knead the dough on a floured surface until smooth and roll into a ball. Cover in plastic wrap and set aside at room temperature for 30 minutes.

Divide the pastry into 12 equal pieces. Roll each piece into a ball and roll out into a circle of 15 cm. Divide this circle into two equal pieces with a knife.

Brush each edge with a little water, and then form a cone shape with the dough around your fingers, sealing the dampened edge.

Fill the cases with a tablespoon of the meat mixture (or vegetable if it is preferred) and press the two dampened edges together to seal the top of the cone. Deep fry the patties in hot oil until crisp. When brown take out and drain on a cloth.

Seeking Comfort
in Cooking

As the Anglo-Indian family lived together in a small community in Kirkee, they sat down to meal after meal together. Kids were at one table and adults at the other. Yvonne's favorite memories were when she went to her Uncle Paddy and Auntie Kathleen's house and they told her wonderful stories of wild India and funny anecdotes about this Ayre or that business man. Later their sons David and Ivor Stevens played cards and joked with Yvonne's brothers. Yvonne and her brothers adored David and Ivor and they became like older brothers to her family.

"Who will be it?" shouted Gerry. "Collin, you be in the Middle."

David, Ivor, Yvonne, Collin, Gerry, George, and little Reggie played Cricket, Goli and Ghilli, raced toward a mark and then back, played pease-porridge hot-clapping their hands on their knees, bye-bye birdie and other out door games till the sun went down.

All were genuinely healthy in a place where disease ran rampant.

It was rare that any of the boys would be sick, but eventually the shadow of disease cast its long arm on the family. When David Stevens was 10 years old his family's fears of the worst came to fruition. David developed the horrific Typhoid fever. The Typhoid outbreak in India claimed thousands of lives. Some died, while others survived to tell the story of the virulent disease. The family didn't think it would be as bad as it was, but it got worse very quickly, as deadly diseases of India do, and within two weeks David was gone. It was a blow to both Mother and Father, and Gillou, his caregiver as well. His Mother, Kathleen (Auntie Kathleen) barely gained enough strength to leave the house. She thought she might die of sadness. After the grief of losing him she spoke only to Dolly about what it was like to battle the virus and to watch her child die so young.

Auntie Kathleen became withdrawn, and it was her servant girl Gillou that managed to keep her going. If she had to cook for family, no one believes she would have been able to. Gillou and Auntie Millie were there to feed and help her.

In the years that followed the boy's death, the desire to cook consumed Gillou. Auntie Kathleen never cooked as she had Gillou to do that. Anglo-Indians barely ever went into the Kitchen. But she occasionally saw Gillou kneading of the pastry dough. For Gillou it possessed an unexpected healing power, one that ultimately renewed her heart and soul after a difficult day of remembrance of the boy. One of Auntie Kathleen's favorites was Indian Patties for the kids. Gillou planned and then cooked for Auntie's family and sometimes our family. Not only did she prepare spicy Anglo-Indian meals, but also English and Irish meals as well (per Auntie Kathleen's request). And the family ate plate after plate that she prepared.

"How does Gillou know how to prepare such foods?"

"She would listen to my recipes and sometimes ask for the assistance from others," said Auntie Kathleen.

"What do these Indians know about cooking for us?" A British woman once asked Auntie Kathleen. When, in actuality they knew a great deal, since they had been living in India with the British for generations.

Dolly brought her servant girl over occasionally to learn from Gillou and Auntie Millie.

"No, No, use the water in which the rice has been boiled for the puree," said Gillou in Hindi to Dolly's servant girl, Manisha.

"Acha," said Manisha.

"You should also use it for white soups," said Gillou with a sigh, as she turned toward Dolly who was standing on the side with her servant watching Gillou.

"The rice water also makes a pleasant drink, just flavor it with sugar and lemon juice," added Dolly.

Gillou just wanted to cook and cook some more. When Auntie Kathleen wasn't pushing Gillou to cook special English dishes she was encouraging her other son, Ivor to become a better student and an engineer like his father. Paddy worked as an engineer in the *Factory* in Kirkee. She also cared for her husband, who had turned to drinking after his son's death.

Dolly looked at Kathleen. First a smile and then a sad frown covered Dolly's face as she stepped away toward the window. She remembered how her own mother talked with her about food. *England Nana*, as Yvonne would say, preferred the English meals, but ate Indian foods also.

Dolly could still hear her Mum's voice, "Curries, dear, are universal—all across the world. But outside of India it is impossible to find a curry made the proper way," Evelyn used to say. "It's in the curry powder. Genuine Indian curry powder can produce a real Indian curry of the very finest."

And they were the finest curries. Evelyn learned to eat the Indian curries and then have it served just how her husband and children liked it. It was full of flavor, slightly spicy, but not overwhelming, rich and mouth watering.

The servants used to discuss in Hindi in the Kitchen, "Really good curry powder that will keep for years and always produce a perfect curry, is made up of many different seeds, roots, and spices, well chosen, well blended, neither too hot or pungent. Always remember to "Bhoon" it. Bhooning means to fry the curry ingredients tenderly on a slow fire with the onion and garlic for 3 to 4 minutes before adding any other ingredients. Bhooning always gets rid of that raw curry flavor."

She missed her mother and her mother's home sometimes, but knew she couldn't return. Not because her mother didn't get along with her husband—by that time, that was water under the bridge. The reason was because Evelyn and John Rixson had left to reside in England.

A few months earlier, Dolly's Mum had stopped by on the way to England to see her and her kids. The family sat together at dinner and ate a grand English meal, talking about how all was changing in India. As in her mother's reserved fashion, she did not cry nor did Dolly when saying goodbye.

"What shall I call you?" asked Yvonne.

"You can call me *England Nana* and you will come see me one day, Yes?" asked Evelyn.

"Yes, Nana," said Yvonne and they hugged gently goodbye.

So now, listening in on conversations between Kathleen, Millie, and Florence, Dolly smiled. "This will always be my home and Florence will always be like a mother to me." said Dolly to herself.

"Aye, what are you doing with that, you don't add those 2 ingredients together." Gillou cried grabbing the bag away from Manisha. "Sultanas and almonds should never be added to the curry."

"But, Gillou it is for the English to eat," Manisha stressed while turning her head from side-to-side as she always did.

"Manisha, come here. Sit down," said Gillou in Hindi.

"Some dishes you need to make the Anglo-Indian way," said Gillou.

Gillou explained that every ingredient in the Indian curry powder that they made on the curry stone in their humble back room has a rich history.. "That is what we will serve here. The English loved it then, they grew up on it, and you will continue. We don't want to change what they are doing, just a little more spicy and pungent... and never sultanas. I'll show you how."

On an afternoon of cooking, the aroma of the freshest green coriander mixed with green ginger filled the room. From the kitchen, Dolly heard the Hindi phrases for "never this and always that" repeated over and over when she visited Kathleen's and Millie's kitchens. The words "Boghar, Bhoon, Dhum, Ghee, Tamarind, and Thainga also echoed in her mind. They were all important words to know in the Anglo-Indian kitchen. The happy sounds were as pleasant to her ears as they were to her tongue.

On special cooking days, the servants would make one of Dolly's favorites, Irish Stew, just like she ate with her Mum. But, today they were creating her other Indian favorite — Kooftah curry and Biryani.

Kooftah was largely favored throughout India, but especially so in central India. It is a dish of minced mutton (or beef) blended with onions, garlic, ginger and spices and cooked in a light curry sauce.

Anglo-Goanese Kooftah Curry

   1 ounce of ghee lightly fried for 3 or 4 minutes
   1 onion and 2 cloves of garlic (chopped finely)
   2 or 3 fresh pickled chilies, cut lengthwise in halves.

Mix into this a dessert-spoonful of curry power and tea-spoonful of tomato paste, and continue the slow cooking for another 2 or 3 minutes. Then with a little water, convert this into a thickish gravy. Salt and lemon juice to taste. Bring to a boil, and then simmer it.

Take 1 lb. of sausage meat and with slightly floured hands, make into small balls the size of large marbles and drop them, one by one, into the simmering sauce.

Do not stir, but shake the pan gently now and again to prevent the balls from caking together.

Dolly's family ate this Kooftah with another Anglo-Indian dish called Biryani on the side.

Irish Stew (Anglo-Indian style)

> 3 lbs beef or mutton cut into medium-sized chunks
> 1 cup carrots cut into large chunks
> 1 1/2 cup potatoes, cut in quarters
> 1/2 cup celery
> 1/4 cup chopped green onions
> 1/4 cup cauliflower
> 2 tbsp vegetable oil
> Salt and fresh ground black pepper to taste
> 1 tbsp butter
> 1 onion, chopped
> 3 tbsp flour for broth
> 3 tbsp flour to season meat
> 1 1/2 cups beef broth
> 1 1/2 cups cow's milk
> 1/4 cup cocoanut milk (grate cocoanut and then moisten with water, place on fire, bring to a boil and then press through a strainer to get the milk)
> 1/2 tsp dried rosemary

Wash the meat and vegetables. Season the meat with salt and ground black pepper and flour. Add the vegetable oil to a heavy pot on medium-high heat. When it begins to heat up, add the meat and brown very well on both sides. Once browned, remove it carefully and set aside.

Reduce the heat to medium, and add the onions. Sauté the onions until softened. Reduce the heat to medium-low, add the butter and remaining flour, and cook for 1 minute stirring often. Stir in the cow's milk, broth, and cocoanut milk. The flour will start to thicken the liquid as it comes to a simmer. Add the rosemary.

Add the rest of the ingredients, except for the potatoes. Add the meat back in, cover, and simmer on low heat for 1 1/2 hours. Add the potatoes, 1 tsp salt, and continue to cook until the potatoes are tender and the beef or mutton is falling off the bones. Stir in the green onions.

Taste and serve hot. The gravy should have a "light" brown appearance when served.

A Servant's Prideful Gestures

During the early 20th century success and pride for middle class Anglo-Indian families were their homes. Although rented, they took great pride in them. First they searched for homes that were near their family and friends, then if they were solidly built. Then, to proclaim their financial worth, they proceeded to heavily decorate these homes with cherry wood furniture, fine fabric and drapes. Without a doubt, servants must be running about as a testament of wealth and worth. The number of servants depended on one's income. In their minds, it was necessary to sustain their way of living and most importantly their way of eating.

Drawing from British tradition, the Anglo-Indian way of cooking always had more meat in it, as opposed to the Indian way, which had more vegetables. Yvonne's family typically had meat everyday—beef, lamb, or goat. And fowl was served for "high-holy days" as James' mother would say.

When Yvonne was a child, just before a feast day, Yvonne's father James would buy a full live fowl to make chicken curry, or one of the English recipes Florence was handed down. Then he would kill and unfeather it, while his sons watched wide-eyed from the side. The servants would drain, clean and then cook it. They hung it up overnight on a string and the blood would drain out completely.

Florence (Yvonne's India Nana) had her daughter Millie cook the meals, then send it over in a Tiffin Carrier. Millie would teach the servants how to prepare the meals appropriately for the families, and so on and so on. The servants taught their daughters and friends how to cook and how to make many Anglo-Indian meat dishes. They did this so their daughters would have a valuable and desirable skill that would get them hired. To be able to tell a potential employer that you could cook English and Anglo-Indian meals was very important.

Millie lived down the street from Dolly and Florence and the men, women and kids often went from one house to another.

"Ayre?" Millie would call out to the cook.

Their female cook was frequently called "Ayre" and her husband was called "Boy". At this time in India, this was not meant in a derogatory way, but used out of tradition and familiarity.

Just before one of the feast days Millie coached Ayre about the week ahead. "Come here Ayre. I want to talk with you about dinner for this weekend. I want you to get 2 pounds of mutton, 3 lbs of beef and goat meat," Millie said.

The cook listened attentively.

Employing servants in India was a responsibility and in many cases a blessing for both the servant and the family served. Yvonne's parents and aunts and uncles had the responsibility for most of the servants they employed by taking them in, feeding them, clothing them as much as the servants themselves had the responsibility of taking care of the family. Auntie Millie, Auntie Kathleen and Yvonne's grandmother had several servants, among which they developed some long lasting relationships.

When Yvonne was young, Maina was the servant woman in her grandmother Florence's house. Yvonne and the family called her Ayre. Ayre would do most of the cooking for her grandmother. When Yvonne lived with her grandmother

Florence, she was discouraged from watching Ayre in the kitchen, so she never learned how to cook full meals while in India.

Mait Rani cleaned the toilets. She was an untouchable. The practice of untouchability was moving toward abolishment, but citizens from all over the country still treated a certain caste of people as though they were beneath them.

Dhoby was the laundry woman. She came once per week to gather the clothes, then wash, press, fold and bring the clothes back to the house.

They also had two part-time servants. Bandhu, the gardener and handyman was the last to join the family, after the other gardener had passed away. He and his wife Prama came into the house as a team. As the years went by Bandhu, Prama and later their two strapping sons became part of the family. Bandhu and Prama and stayed as a team with the family until they shifted residence in 1930 and Prama stopped coming to work. Bandhu however continued and stayed with the family. Through his time their Bandhu looked after the small garden, kept the grounds and outside house clean, got horses or rickshaws for the women or men to take to town, and ran errands for Florence or Kathleen, as well as attended to small odd jobs at home as needed.

Bandhu took pride in his work, and became very possessive about the home, the garden, the horses or rickshaw--and later the car, and just about anything pertaining to Yvonne and her extended family. In later years, Yvonne learned that she had to be extremely careful in getting things done by others as he insisted on the right of first refusal. Knowing his limitations, this was quite complicated for Yvonne at times, but his sensibilities had to be taken into account and he be given a role in the task. Take for instance some carpentry or plumbing work to be done at home. If James contacted either a plumber or a carpenter without Bandhu's acting as the intermediary, Bandhu would sulk. So, they inevitably always got Bandhu to call on such experts to come and do what was needed to be done under his own supervision.

Another memorable servant was Tarla, who stayed with Florence almost 15 years. She swept and swabbed all the floors of their home, washed all the dishes and vessels, and helped put away all the clothes.

As she got older, Tarla eventually evolved to be a full-fledged Indian housewife in her own home. Between her own household schedule and some bouts with illness, Tarla's time with the family grew less and less. On the days that she could not come, Auntie Kathleen's servant girl Raina was sometimes called to come to the house and handle the home maker jobs and do all the work that Tarla normally did. When Raina covered for Tarla this was an inconvenience to Auntie Kathleen, because then work would not get done at Auntie Kathleen's house.

Maybe the most important servant was Kashwini, who was completely dedicated to helping Auntie Millie with the cooking. And she became an *amazing* cook herself. She lived in the back of Florence's house with her husband Hiresh, who did work around the house as well. Yvonne was told to call him Boy and Kashwini Ayre. They were irreplaceable in their lives and both cared for the family as they cared for each other.

Florence also employed a messenger, whom all called Peon (pronounced Peun). He would ride a bike into town, post letters, and carry Tiffin carriers (lunch boxes) to and from Yvonne's grandmother's house to her mother's house or Auntie Kathleen's house down the road.

In India, sweets were typically eaten more or less as food for nourishment rather than simple sugar confections. They were very rich, nourishing snacks and had ingredients such as ghee, and coa, dhood, soojee and badura. Adults and kids alike found that they were tasty and very sustaining. The top "sweets and sweetmeats" in the LeStyne house were Hulwas, Luddoos, Burfis, Coa, Dhood-padah, Goolab jamon, and Jellabies.

Sweets were complex and involved a lot of work to make. Kashwini or Auntie Millie would usually be too busy with other chores and food preparation to spend the time it took to make them. But still, they did manage to find time and make them once per month or for a special occasion. At other times, Dolly, Florence, or Auntie Kathleen, usually bought these at the bazaar, fairs or railway stations.

One of Yvonne's favorite dishes as a young child was the very Anglo-Indian treat of Banana Fritters. Auntie Millie was sure to make them at least once per month for little Yvonne and especially on her birthday.

Millie would use two large ripe bananas mashed into a pulp and add a thick batter made of ¼ cup flour and 2 eggs, together with a little cow's milk. She mixed it well and then dropped a dessert-spoonful of the mixture into deep boiling fat. It was cooked to a golden brown, drained and then served well dusted with castor sugar.

Christians in India

The times of the year that all the Anglo-Indian aunts and uncles and cousins got together were Christmas and Easter. On these high-holy days, Yvonne's parents, paternal grandparents, and brothers sat down for a big meal: many English meals were served, but there were also chapatis and parathas with curry or sometimes just rice with the curry on the table. Dal was also served to them with rice and they ate that with delight at family gatherings.

While the family was Anglo-Indian, they were also Roman Catholic-Christian and went to church to celebrate the high holy days. Indian Christians and Anglo-Indian Christians were not considered the same by people within the Anglo-Indian community. The Anglo-Indians thought of themselves as Christians by origin and the Indian Christians as Christians who have converted.

But, the family all gathered at these two Christian holidays and did not only have just curry and rice on the table, but also served Dolly's favorite Irish Stew.

Yvonne's Portuguese grandparents—Florence and George also celebrated these holidays and went to mass on Sunday.

Yvonne's grandfather would sit and tell all the stories, but the kids rarely listened in, but instead ran off playing cricket and gilly-don-dou.

The history of Portuguese missionaries in India started with apostles who landed in 1498 along with the Portuguese explorer Vasco da Gama who was seeking to form alliances with pre-existing Christian nations. When he and the Portuguese missionaries arrived they found no Christians in the country, except in the area of Malabar. These were a special sect of Christians known as St. Thomas Christians. The St. Thomas Christians were friendly to the Portuguese missionaries at first and they and the other Christians mingled and managed well together for many years. Eventually Portuguese missionaries established a Portuguese Mission in 1500 and got permission from the Kochi Raja to build two churches - Santa Cruz Basilica and St. Francis Church— using stones and mortar which was almost unheard of at that time as the local prejudices were against such a structure for any purpose other than a royal palace or a temple.

Between the 1500s and the 1900s the Church and its charities grew exponentially. It then flat lined after the Depression. One of the by-products of this Christian era in the 1900s was Mother Teresa's ministry.

Sister Teresa (later Mother Teresa), arrived in India in 1929, the same year Yvonne was born. Sister Teresa began her work in Darjeeling, near the Himalayan mountains where she learnt Bengali and taught at a school close to her convent called St. Teresa's School.

Although Sister Teresa enjoyed teaching, she was increasingly disturbed by the poverty surrounding her in Calcutta. The Bengal famine of 1943 brought horror and despair to the city, and the outbreak of Hindu/Muslim violence in August 1946 plummeted the city into more desolation.

Yvonne hadn't heard of Sister Teresa *or Mother Teresa* until she was a young teenager. Once she did she was enthralled. She took every chance she had to read about the woman or listened for news about her on the radio. Her mother and grandmother revered Mother Teresa as well. Young Yvonne and her friends from Breach Candy School admired her. She was something similar to a Hollywood star to her age group.

Mother Teresa was devoutly Catholic and devoted to Jesus. She would express her ceaseless devotion in many ways. It was inevitable for Christians in India to hear about her. The thing that brought her to "everyman" though was her respect for all religions and her strong need for all people of India to come closer to God. She once wrote, "We should help a Hindu become a better Hindu, a Muslim become a better Muslim, a Catholic become a better Catholic," and finished with her most powerful advice "Everything starts with Prayer."

Auntie Devereux
comes to Poona

The year is now 1943 and Yvonne, a teenager, always tries to be the best Christian she can be, but sometimes it is hard. It was in that year that her mother's Aunt Edith Devereux came to visit.

"Who is she, Mum?" asked Yvonne, while her younger brothers listened.

"She is your Aunt Edith and she is very British," said Dolly. "We must be on our best behavior and help her with anything she needs while she is here. Is that understood?" Dolly said sternly to all the children.

"Yes, Mother of course," said Yvonne not really knowing how this British woman was different from other British women she had met so many other times around Kirkee and Poona.

Dolly's Aunt Edith Devereux was her father Alfred's sister. She was rich, bossy and if in England, she would have been a noblewoman thought Yvonne, but in India she was less than that. Dolly had grown up with hearing about the importance of class in her culture and so of course, by now shared the same conception of the importance of class with her mother, and among others in her family. They all believed in the dignity of lineage, but to Dolly it was less relevant than to the others. Despite her fears about Aunt Edith's attitudes, out of a sense of family loyalty, Dolly accepted the request of Edith and John to come stay with her for a few weeks while they got settled in Poona.

From Edith Devereux's first arrival, her behavior was wrought with class snobbery and disdain, especially in her attempts at ordering her niece Dolly around.

"Dolly, HELP me with this." or "Dolly, please get someone to fetch me this."

This also was vivid when helping Edith prepare for her and her husband's move to Poona. Edith's husband John was offered and accepted a job in the military in Poona and there were numerous things to get settled before he started.

The lines of class in India were strictly drawn, but rarely ever seen by young Yvonne at this perspective. These lines were never as obvious to Dolly and Yvonne as when Dolly's Aunt Edith arrived from Calcutta with her husband that spring.

Caste and class in India ran from the untouchables to the upper classes. With the class system in India a person could rarely climb up and down the social ladder, but that did not mean acceptance by the other class. Class was intricately related to reputation and status in India, as it was in England, in that both reflect the strictly regimented nature of life for the middle and upper-middle classes and the Anglo-Indians and British. While the LeStynes, who were middle class, might socialize with Devereuxs, they were clearly treated as their social inferiors.

The days turned into weeks and before long Aunt Edith was warming up to her surroundings with the LeStynes. The servants were cooking for her, and cleaning and helping her directly in every way. Yvonne had to run errands every day and be on call every night for any other tasks that Aunt Edith wished for.

Feeling so comfortable, yet lonely for her own friendship with people within her own type of social class, Edith called on a group of her friends to come one evening to visit at the LeStyne house while she and her husband were there.

"Dolly, you should make only English meals and we want you to have all the servants wear black and white, none of this garb that you have them running around in now," ordered Edith.

"Are you sure? Will your friends really mind?" questioned Dolly.

"*I* will mind. Of course they will mind" said Edith. "Please have it done."

"Yes, Auntie. I will make sure it is done," said Dolly.

"And the kids. I want you to make sure the children are in bed by the time my guests arrive. The Carsons are not really used to seeing such dark Anglo-Indian children.

There was silence when Dolly lowered her eyes and then raised them again.

"Yes. I'll make sure they are asleep," Dolly said.

"Even Yvonne," said Edith.

"Even Yvonne?" asked Dolly.

"Yes," said Edith.

Dolly decided at that moment not to tell Yvonne till the day of the party.

The day of the party arrived and when she heard she was shocked by the news.

"Mom, you must be daft? All of us must leave because we are too dark? Why must I go? I am the oldest. I'm as old as some of these girls that are coming," said Yvonne. She dared not also add that she was as light as the girls who were coming.

"Just do it. I don't want to hear any back talk," said Dolly.

"No Mum. I won't," said Yvonne.

"You absolutely must," said Dolly.

"I will not. Tell her no," said Yvonne.

Upon hearing that from the other room, Edith walked in the room and looked Yvonne in the eye and said "Yes, you will dear and with no arguments."

Yvonne turned around furiously and left the room. When she went upstairs she screamed and cried in her pillow, cursing Edith in the silence of her room.

Later, because guilt was a way of life in Catholicism, Yvonne felt horribly guilty the next day about her words and attitude toward her family, not to mention cursing her aunt. She felt so guilty in fact that the next time she went to confession she wanted to make a point of asking forgiveness.

Confession

One ritual that Catholics, Protestants and other Christians practiced was the ritual of confession. It was a sunny, warm morning when Yvonne, walked to the church near her mother's home to go to confession. This was not unusual, as she often would need to do confession midweek.

Upon getting there, she said "Father, please forgive me for I have sinned."

"Wait," said Father John.

"Yes Father," said Yvonne holding her breath.

"You are not to say another word," said Father John.

"Yes, Father," Yvonne said, thinking to herself, "What have I done?"

"You must go home immediately and not return like this," he said.

"Sorry father, what is it that angers you?" gasped Yvonne.

"You, my dear are not dressed appropriately," he said.

She quickly looked down at what she was wearing.

The skirt was beyond the knee and the blouse had short sleeves which bared only a portion of her upper arms.

"..showing your arms," said the Priest.

Stunned and embarrassed for a second at the priest's reaction, she just answered obediently, "Oh.. I, I am so sorry Father. I will go home immediately and change." At the same time, in her mind she thought of all the girls that went around with far less clothing than this everyday.

When she returned home, she was furious.

"Why are you back so soon?" asked her grandmother, Florence.

"Oh my Goodness!" Yvonne exclaimed as she flapped her arms down at her sides in exasperation.

"What happened?" asked Florence.

"I can't believe it. I am never going back to that church again. I'm so embarrassed," Yvonne cried out as she entered the door. She proceeded to tell her grandmother and cousin about what took place at the church.

"Well, you must do confession," said her grandmother.

"I will go another day this week. I can't go back there again today." she said.

"It's hot out there. I think it's better not to obsess over outward appearances but concentrate on the condition of our soul. Why can't we dress properly for the weather?" Yvonne asked rhetorically.

When she returned again for confession 4 days later in the 99 degree heat she wore a long sleeved dress.

"Father, forgive me for I have sinned…" started Yvonne.

The Boarding
School life...

Earlier in her life, when Yvonne was about 5 years old her grandmother Florence wanted to put her in an appropriate school for girls. She saw promise and intelligence in Yvonne. But, living far from the city, there were few, if any options.

"There are no good schools in Kirkee," said Dolly. "But where will she go?"

"How about Jesus Saint Mary Convent school, which is run by the nuns?" asked Florence.

"We can't afford that I'm sure," said Dolly.

"Yes, we can. My father would role over in his grave if he heard that one of his great grandchildren were not able to attend that school," said Florence.

"Dolly, Yvonne's great grandfather, Sir Michael DeQuadros was knighted by the Queen because he did charity work in Bombay and built the first Jesus and Mary convent in Bombay, and then later supported it financially." said Florence.

"Well, yes, replied Dolly. In that case then I am fine with Yvonne going to the girl's boarding school associated with the Convent of Jesus and Mary," she said. "If it is possible, but we are paying for the boys to be in elementary school. We can't afford to pay for Yvonne as well."

That afternoon, Florence didn't think twice about writing a letter to the headmistress about requesting her granddaughter attend the school.

Within two weeks Florence heard back from the headmistress telling her to send the young girl with her mother to the
school and that they would take her tuition-free.

"Dolly, no one will have to pay," said Florence. "And it is
all girls."

"I can't believe it. Even though it was Yvonne's great
grandfather, she got in free," said Florence.

"That's wonderful. Wait till I tell the family," said Dolly.

The schools of Jesus and Mary all had a powerful brand
name in India from the onset. The 1st Jesus and Mary was
built in Bombay. Another was built in Poona. Later, there was
another one built in Agra.

So in 1936, Yvonne went to **Jesus Saint Mary** convent
school in Poona. Her mother and grandmother both decided
to allow her to board there as well. She studied reading, writing,
and arithmetic, and developed many long lasting friendships.
Although it was only 7 miles away from where her mother and
grandmother lived Yvonne rarely came home, except for holidays and sick time.

Yvonne's attendance at this school created the greatest
sense of pride in the family—more than they had felt in a long
time. The legacy of the Convent of Jesus and Mary School
went back to British-colonial times.

Yvonne's school was the first in a chain of Jesus and Mary
Schools to be set up in Western India.

Long before Yvonne's time there, in 1904, the school was
shifted to a two storied building adjoining the 'Holy Name
Cathedral' at Wodehouse Road. The two-storied building with
its airy and spacious corridors was sought after by many parents. The school began to grow rapidly and as expected, it was
decided to eventually construct a proper school building with
dormitories. The majestic porch served as both the entry and
departure points. It has seen many little girls entering the por-
tals with tears, and then well groomed teenagers leaving with
confident eyes. It was a second home for Yvonne for years.

Over the years the school grew and changed as the children grew and changed themselves. The progress and development of the school was always marked by a harmonious blend of traditions, from both the East and the West.

In the years Yvonne was there, Mother Superior Blandeine took personal responsibility to educate children of the Catholic community and offer them well-rounded training in academics and character development, while respecting the Indian traditions and native people.

Educating Yvonne

Back in the 1930s when Yvonne and her brothers were getting ready for Primary school, there were about 316 primary and secondary schools, 180 boarding schools and 136 day schools for Anglo-Indians to attend in India.

Most of what were considered "first-class" schools were run by Anglo-Indians or by British nuns, because they spoke English "well" and reportedly "provided a superior westernized" education. The British nuns almost always hired Anglo-Indians to be teachers and assistants at the schools and hostiles.

Most of Yvonne's Anglo-Indian relatives or friends worked or had worked within the private schools, the telegraph, post office, or in the railway industry, because these were owned and run by the British. If not, the working men were likely in the ranks of the military.

As the Depression riled on, it became harder and harder for all of Yvonne's younger brothers to attend private school, or any school for that matter. It was more important to feed and secure the family.

A well-respected government group was commissioned in 1945 to study how far Anglo-Indian children go in school. This was research done on children right before, during, and after the depression, which included Yvonne, her brothers, and her cousins. The researchers came to the conclusion that out of every 100 Anglo-Indian children in the lowest class, 83 proceeded to middle school, 45 to high school, 5 to intermediate school or got a Cambridge HS certificate and only 2 went on to the university degree level.

It turns out that Yvonne's siblings' and cousins' education levels closely mirrored the study, although they were middle class. Yvonne went on to high school, then on to finish an Intermediate teaching degree. One of her brothers went to high school. All of her other brothers and cousins went as far as middle school. Only her cousin Ivor Stevens (Auntie Kathleen's remaining son) went on to University, where he received a degree in Civil Engineering. Ivor eventually was given an opportunity in South Africa and ended up managing one of the largest bridge-building projects on the African continent at that time.

Anglo-Indian fathers, like James and Paddy (Ivor's father), struggled to obtain and keep jobs to put their kids through private schools or to stay in the railway schools. But, the average income in 1945 was 150 to 200 rupees per month. It had been even less in the 1930s. Because of the high cost of education, Anglo-Indian parents found it hard to continue education in private institutions.

Anglo-Indians filled the railway employment ranks and their children filled the railway schools. Ivor eventually went to the University with some boys who had been through the railway schools. There were 69 railway schools in the 1940s for Anglo Indians to attend —62 were primary, 4 middle and 3 high schools.

In addition, compulsory enlistment in the military's Auxiliary Force was a pre-condition for employment of Anglo-Indians in the railways. The railway battalions formed the backbone of the Auxiliary Force. Apart from being called out to protect the railway property against arson and looting by strikers the auxiliary force was also called out for military duty to quell the riots of the time. This group was responsible for doing duty as a second line of defense and serve as an auxiliary to the standing army.

In 1928 the auxiliary force was made up of over 2/3rds Anglo-Indians---the rest were the Domiciled Europeans or Europeans. Only 110 of them were given commissions.[11] The other armed force at the time was the Indian Territorial Force. In that organization every officer, except a commandant, and an adjutant, was an Indian. Both of these forces eventually merged into the IDF (Indian Defense Force) then the AFI – Auxiliary force of India.

The Auxiliary Force reportedly, demonstrated some of the worst examples of the official British policies of discrimination according to Frank Anthony of the Anglo Indian Association. These awful policies were manifested when the British promoted and favored those who were from Britain, over those Anglo-Indians already in the community, primarily because of the political unrest throughout India.

In the Anglo-Indian schools of Yvonne's teenage years, history, arithmetic and literature were required. Yvonne encountered lessons about European nations, predominantly the British Empire, but also the history of India and the rise and fall of the Mughal Empire. Knowledge of Bahadur Shah Zafar and his Mughal ancestors and how they interacted with the East India Company was imperative reading for an educated Anglo-Indian in India. It was also compulsory to learn how to read and write English and Hindi.

By the mid 1930s the Indian government made it compulsory for the teaching of Indian languages from the primary to high school years. Yvonne was required to learn how to read and write Hindi, as were all of her younger brothers. It was more difficult for her as she was not taught it from a young age. She and her siblings required tutors because they did not speak Hindi at home, but only a little with the servants and in town when necessary. Her grandparents managed to learn it and spoke well enough to get by and Yvonne remembered some phrases here and there from them.

Hindi is a modern Indo-Aryan language prevalently spoken in South Asian countries, such as India, Pakistan and Nepal, as well as other countries outside Asia (South Africa, Trinidad, etc). Thus, it was the likely choice for Anglo-Indians such as Yvonne and her brothers to learn.

Hindi is the descendant of the Sanskrit language, synonymous with Hindui, Hindawi, Rexta, and Rexti. The terms Urdu and Hindustani are also used to refer to the language. However Urdu and Hindi actually denote a mixed speech spoken around the area of Delhi, in Northern India which gained popularity between the Arabs and Afghans and native residents.

Yvonne had to practice Hindi everyday. In writing the Devanagari script, she wrote from left to right and from the top of the page down. She always spoke out loud when writing, because the script was phonetic in nature and there was a regular correspondence between the letters and their pronunciation. Unlike English, in Hindi there were no upper case and lower case letters.

Ka, ga, gHa", she tried initially. These consonants were called velar because the back of the tongue touched the rear of the soft palate or vellum. They were similar to the English k and g. Hindi retains that distinction between aspirated and unaspirated consonants, which results in a four-way contrast.

"Kal, Khal, gal, ghal, Tal, tal…" she repeated over and over until larger words were clearly formed and then sentences were formed, followed by an ability to have a dialog and then for her final exam to say an entire story in Hindi.

As she grew older Hindi became a necessity in the everyday lives of Yvonne and her friends and family.

Vocabulary on the body, health, ailments, then colors, family and relatives, food and drink, numbers and currency, time and important verbs were mandatory for all her friends, brothers and cousins still in school.

Yvonne may have learned about currency early on through her parents and relatives, but it was also compulsory for Anglo-

Indians to know about the Indian national currency and other European currencies through their mathematics studies. Rupees were the common form of currency in British India. A paisa was equal to two dhelas, three pies and six damarees. Other coins were two paisas (taka), two annas (dawannee), four annas (a chawanee, or a quarter of a rupee), and eight annas.

Before long her instructors found that English words were being nativized into Hindi and they had their own pronunciation with an Indian tongue. Yvonne often spoke these modified words with ease, running these English terms into the conversation, like bringing a friend into the room.

Yvonne and her brothers listened to servants and watched Indian films to be able to improve their dialog. She understood by the time she was 14 what was generally being said, but rarely used it in fear that she would say something wrong.

It wasn't till she was about 16 and wanted to try out her Hindi in a Sari shop to get a sari for herself that she could confidently speak it. Yvonne and her girlfriends found more and more that Hindi was a necessity to bargain or negotiate, but sometimes it was very complex. Here is one example:

Yvonne: zara naye fashion ki sari dikaiye. (Please show me a sari that is in fashion)

ShopKeeper: kaun si sari cahiye? Reshmi ya suti? (what kind of saree do you want?)

Yvonne: reshmi (silk)

ShopKeeper: ye dekiye. Aj-kal is ka bahut rivaj he. (Look at this. Nowadays it is very much the custom/fashion)

dekiye, silk kitna accah he! (see how good the silk is?)

The shop woman begins to show Yvonne a few sarees in various colors.

Yvonne: ye pili. (I want the yellow one)

Yvonne: is ka dam kya he? (what is the price?)

Shopkeeper: bara sau rupees. (1200 rupees)

Yvonne: Tik Bataiye, ye bahar se ayi he. (please tell me the right price. It is for a friend that is not from here—in a tone that requested a discount)

Shopkeeper: aj-kal itna dam he…acca gyara sau. (This is the price nowadays…okay, eleven hundred rupees)

Yvonne: acc a Tik he.(okay, that is fine.)

Cycling Through
The City

For centuries the human rickshaw was a popular mode of transportation in India. A human-pulled rickshaw is the type of transport wherein a person pulls a small cart by hand. In other words, a man, instead of a horse, pulls and runs with people inside the small rickshaw carriage. By 1940 human rickshaw were replaced to a great extent with the Cycle rickshaws, largely out of convenience. They were bigger than a tricycle where two people sit on an elevated seat at the back and a person pedals on a cycle from the front. Cycle rickshaws progressed to be a steadfast sight on the streets of Delhi and Bombay streets by India's independence in 1947. It provided the cheapest way around the cities.

Cycles were just another form of transportation for the family. In India, the word "bike" generally refers to motorcycle, and "cycle" refers to bicycle. Bicycles were also used as a common mode of travel in much of India, especially for the younger generation. Along with walking, cycling accounted for almost 75% of the traveling and commuting to and from work and school for Yvonne, her father, brothers and cousins throughout the streets of Kirkee, Poona and Bombay.

It was this backdrop, throughout these Central Indian towns, in which accidents tended to happen. Thousands of people traveled the streets of Poona on rickshaw, bike, car or by foot. The mix of traffic, throngs of pedestrians and lack of traffic lights created a picture like no other place in the world.

One morning, James and his 10 year old daughter Yvonne left early for the city on their cycle. Yvonne was returning to school after her summer vacation and James wanted to drop her off then try to make it to work within the hour. Their cycle had been through many miles. It was a cloudy day in July and a monsoon rain had just ended the day prior. The roads were slicker than usual. The spokes of this bike, as with other bikes, do much of the work. First, spokes don't push outward like it might seem. Rather, the rim is evenly pulled inward by spokes that are laced through the hub, and the center part of the wheel that rotates around the axle, which makes it extraordinarily strong. These spokes coming from the hub then radiate outward to the rim. The spokes played a key role in transferring the power from James' legs to the rim to make the bike go. Enormous force was applied to the hub of the rear wheel by the chain and gearing when he pedaled down hard, and together the spokes carried the power that went from his legs to the chain, then out to the wheel. That force drove the bike forward and energy distributed among many spokes in the properly aligned wheel. Even under a very heavy load the spokes help spread out the weight so that it is more evenly carried and doesn't put too much stress on any single spoke.

Yvonne was riding on the front bars and James was in the rider's seat. She felt the light touch of the front wheel against her small foot as she did on other mornings that she went out with her brother or father like this. Yvonne and James were on the cycle, riding north along Gymkhana Road in Poona when a man on another bike emerged from a side road colliding with them, sending them skidding into the mud. James was unable to take evasive actions, resulting in a crushing collision with the vehicle.

The accident knocked Yvonne off the bike and forced her entire leg and hip to get mangled into the wheels of the bike.

Swiftly her legs got caught in the rotating wheel's spokes, and were crushed against the frame. James was thrown over the top of other rider's bike into the air, landing heavily on the ground.

Yvonne suffered injuries to the forehead, chin and nose. However, it was the spike that went though her calf that caused the greatest damage. She was shocked and silent in pain, as the emergency workers came for her and rushed her to the hospital.

She was medically examined by a doctor who stated that she must get the spike removed immediately and then prepare for a blood transfusion.

Sitting in the hospital Yvonne was given pain killers and her injury taken care of. The hospital released her within a few days.

She returned to school shortly after and caught up with her studies.

The next week she returned to the traffic of the city. Bustling, moving, growing …

Typhoid's Wrath Hits Again

Typhoid illnesses spread throughout Asia with a hellish force during the 1800s and early 1900s.

It was only in the mid-19th century that physicians began to distinguish typhus from malaria. Typhoid fever was frequently associated with military campaigns. With recognition that fecal contamination of food and water supplies was the main mode of transmission of the illness, measures were finally taken to prevent typhoid.

It wasn't till the 20th century that Typhoid fever was starting to get under control throughout the world, to just be localized epidemics. However, India was still a hot spot.

Yvonne's brother, George LeStyne had almost died of it at 5 years old and now another one of Dolly's children was facing death.

When 13-year-old Yvonne was brought to the emergency department of Nehru Medical Hospital in India, with a history of fever for 3 days, they checked her for Typhoid fever immediately. She complained of a severe headache but had no vomiting or blurring of vision. She was febrile with a temperature 39.2°C, looked ill, and her examination revealed mild pallor and a coated tongue. Neurological examination showed her to be conscious and orientated, but with bouts of irrelevant and emotional crying. Doctors said that she had severe impairment with regard to naming and she was repeating words and phrases.

"Papa, I can't swim. I can't swim," she repeated over and over in her delirium.

At that point her father James, summoned the Peon who had accompanied them to the hospital.

"Peon go to our house and tell them of Yvonne's condition," James cried out.

At that moment, the Peun and James witnessed Yvonne collapse, and her breathing came to a near standstill.

Doctors and nurses ran in, while the Peun stood outside the door and watched with pupils dilated. He and all the servants in the family were very fond of Miss Yvonne.

"Should I leave?" he thought. He stood and watched as nurses came in and out. He thought one of them said she had passed. He saw Sire James emotional and crying and did not want to disturb this moment.

He did as James requested originally and took off on his rickshaw toward Kirkee to Elephantson road.

The Typhoid cases were relatively high at this time. The young doctor had seen about 40 cases that year so far and all among kids 2–15 year-olds. Almost all had been from contaminated drinking water in India or Pakistan.

"The disease can last about 2 to 3 weeks, during which time bacteria invades and spreads throughout all your body. The first week of the disease is characterized by high temperatures. The second week begins rose spots and abdominal pain. The third week is marked by more intense intestinal problems, which can result in hemorrhage," the doctor explained to James.

This was before the availability of vaccines for Typhoid. The disease was a burden and one that could hit relatively clean unpopulated areas in India as well as densely populated, unkempt cities.

A typhoid episode consisted of a fever lasting about 3 or more days in a person and if his or her blood was checked they would have a confirmed infected blood culture. Yvonne's blood culture was sent on the day of admission. It showed the growth of S. typhi (*S. paratyphi*): meaning typhoid was spreading.

Peon, the Rickshaw driver finally arrived at Yvonne's mother's house to give the message to Dolly. Sweat was dripping from his face and his heart racing.

"Mamsi, it is terrible news. Yvonne is dying," he said in Hindi. "She is near death. She is very sick and delirious."

"Gerald, what is he saying?" screamed Dolly. Screaming and crying swept throughout the house immediately.

A blow of sickness rolled over Dolly's body, while her face filled with tears. In her anguish she told the Peun to go and get Yvonne's grandmother.

The peun had communicated the story to Florence but with even more remorse…"She is nearing death. It is her last moments," he said again in Hindi.

In a few minutes, Florence and her servant's husband came running into Dolly's house crying and screaming. Within 20 minutes all of her relatives had heard and were running into the house in hysteria.

Florence couldn't believe her eyes. Dolly appeared to have aged 20 years in 1 hour. The older woman sat wrapped in a blanket on the floor of the bungalow's kitchen, surrounded by her sons and her Muslim servant women. She cried out and looked at the door every time it opened, as if searching for her daughter. She couldn't move.

"Dolly, where is she now?" asked Florence.

"At the hospital," said Dolly in a low, weak voice.

At that moment, Auntie Kathleen entered the back of the veranda and stood by a side pillar to check in on the family. She could not bear to hear the news, and lose her favorite niece as she had lost her son exactly the same way years ago.

"My God, is she dying?" asked Kathleen.

"Yes, I think so." said Yvonne's brother to Kathleen.

"No...No," said Dolly. She did not want to believe it.

There were ups and downs and a roller coaster of emotions that followed. The screams came longer and harder.

Finally George said "We should go to the hospital mother."

"I can't watch her die," said Dolly.

"Mum, we must go," said Collin.

"Dolly, I will go with you," said Kathleen. She looked sadly into her eyes and then the two mothers embraced.

"Okay, you all go and I will stay here with the children," said Florence.

"Please go get Bandhu to bring the rickshaw," George commanded the Peon.

Dolly barely remembered the ride to the hospital, not being able to verbalize the pain, to talk about her daughter or respond to any requests.

For Auntie Kathleen and Dolly, the experience of caring for children changed them profoundly in ways often unforeseen. Child rearing affected Dolly deeply, altering not only her lifestyle and her relationships with our husband, but also in the essence of how she thought. She loved her daughter genuinely and could not bear to see her die.

When they arrived at the hospital, the nurse greeted them and informed them that while things were still gravely serious with Yvonne because she was in a Coma, the incident was not as fatal as they originally thought.

"She is still alive and we are trying to keep her such," said the nurse.

"Oh my Gosh...Thank goodness," Dolly and others said relieved. Together they prayed and passed on news to the others by messenger that there was hope.

About 3 months later, Yvonne was out of the coma, back in good health and able to return home.

Conversations
Running Scared

The next week Dolly, met with her friend Kitty.

"My God, thank goodness Yvonne is going to be okay," said Kitty.

"I really scolded the peun for telling me such a fantastic story. I am grateful, but so upset that he had caused such anxiety," said Dolly.

"Oh, my goodness Dolly," said Kitty as she heard Dolly tell her the story. "You do not have to be uneducated to pass such rumors; the educated and rich pass them as well, but even better and with much higher consequences."

"There is hysteria and rumors all around us today, Isn't there?" said Dolly. "The Muslim will kill us all in our sleep, during riots, or poison us while we are most vulnerable and we believe this."

"I think it is because the people who tell them use their uncertainty to make a good story, better," Kitty said.

"I know what you mean. Rumors are all over today. I just can't bear it anymore. Maybe...Maybe these rumors exist because people want to find a way to reduce anxiety or help us find meaning in events they can't understand," said Dolly.

"Yes,...or is it just to improve their social relationships," said Kitty in a joking turn, trying to cheer up her friend. They both smiled because they both knew that social standing was so important in the Anglo-Indian community.

In India, at that time, there was a range of conversational methods that were utilized in diverse ways.

High anxiety was amplified when Muslim and Hindi conversations turned to fighting, and mass riots resulted in deaths. Before long, there was an increase in the internal civil disorder throughout the country. India had obtained its independence from England, the Mother country. As a result, a new conversation emerged within the Anglo Indian community, and it led to a burning question among the Anglo-Indian men and women: **what do we do next?**

Love and Faux Pas

The Asian Indian community in India in the late 40's and early 50's was an ethnically diverse one, to the world looking in. There were a variety of subgroups who trace their roots to different regions or states within India, who spoke different languages, ate different foods, and followed distinctly different customs. The one Dolly and her children came from is the Anglo-Indian (British Raj) sect. Most of the Anglo-Indians were more Anglo than Indian. Only their darker complexions gave away the Indian part of their origins. Otherwise, they dressed like the British, their mother tongue was English (but with an inflection of an Indian accent) and they practiced Christianity. The Anglo-Indian sect didn't typically go out of their way to interact with completely Indian sects such as Sikhs, Punjabis, Bengalis, Hindus or Muslims. However a few times a year they would go to a common gathering place to celebrate important occasions with members of those sub-communities --like the Dawali Indian festival. The older generation of very-British Anglo-Indians did not wear saris or listen to Indian classical music. But, for the younger generation things were different. Their interest slowly assimilated into what the Indian interests were. Yvonne's generation was starting to wear saris to dances and parties and listen to modern western and Indian music, as they understood the Indian languages—especially Hindi, better than their parents.

By this time India was a melting pot of cultures. Yvonne and her friends were learning to be open minded and to accept all the Indian cultures and beliefs.

In 1951, at the age of 21, Yvonne met Rajan. He was 1/2 Hindi and 1/2 Anglo-Indian and she did not think twice of having a friendship with him. Her friends knew his friends. Before long they were taking a few trips to Juhu beach and the Hanging Gardens on Malabar Hill with the group and then with each other.

Dating was more informal than ever before in India. For the first time among Anglo-Indians it was acceptable to not have chaperones on dates between males and females of a certain age. Rajan would sometimes come to the foyer of the boarding school where Yvonne was living, to pick her up. The dates involved considerable freedom, especially if more than one couple attended the outing. Men still picked up the tab and women graciously accepted.

On their dates, Yvonne sometimes wore her best western-style silk dresses, or Indian salva camises and silk saris. Rajan looked handsome in a suit or sometimes the traditional white or formal silk Kurta salwar with matching shawl.

The most popular pastimes for them were dances, horse races, and movies with groups of friends. Before long all of her friends knew that she was in a steady relationship with Rajan and was considering marriage. She had no doubt that he was the one she would marry, and he as well loved her.

They managed to keep their relationship stirring for almost 6 months before he talked to Yvonne about meeting his parents. It was apparent that although she meant a great deal to him he had reservations about introducing his parents to her.

At that time it was common in urban areas and increasingly popular in rural parts, for parents to arrange marriage-aged sons and daughters to meet with multiple potential spouses. And this is what Rajan's parents expected. So when Rajan came home with Yvonne, his mother was immediately not happy. Rajan thought that once his mother met Yvonne she would realize that it was a good match.

It was becoming increasingly common in India for an Anglo-Indian couple whom had met by themselves and was involved romantically to go through the process of an arranged marriage with that specific partner in mind. Since arranged marriages resulted in unifying extended families and were believed to contribute to marital stability, many couples managed their marriages with each other through the processes of an arranged marriage. These marriages were often referred to as self-arranged marriages in India. It was this type of a marriage that Yvonne and Rajan thought best for themselves, but of course with the blessing of their parents.

So, on the night Yvonne met Rajan's parents she looked beautiful in a silk dress to her calf with a matching shawl. Upon picking her up, she saw that Rajan was more nervous than usual. Yvonne remembered to fold her hands and bow, and take off her shoes at the door. Never before had the Hindi language and customs been so critical in Yvonne's life than that night.

Usually the most difficulty Yvonne had with the Hindi language had been with maneuvering verbs and time. She rarely had trouble in addressing elders. The Hindi concept of time was very different from the unilinear concept found in English. Time was not viewed as smoothly flowing from the past through the present into the future. In Hindi, there are instances of finding the present or future within the past.

The expression, "he said that he was going", always was a challenge—it turns out to be "He said that he is going", or "I always went there", was translated as "I always go there" in Hindi.

She did not tell Rajan about her fears about Hindi, because she did not think it would matter so much, as he was so familiar with her and they were so in love.

Upon meeting his mother Ganika, Yvonne handed her a gift with her left hand, not remembering that it was considered very rude (and bad luck) to give something with the left hand.

At the same time, when Rajan introduced her to his mother, Yvonne returned his mother's greeting with a greeting and short conversation, but she accidentally used the wrong form of address to Ganika and her husband. Yvonne chose the incorrect word, and one that instead of indicating respect, was said so incorrectly it was as though she was addressing someone beneath her of a lower caste.

As soon as Yvonne saw the woman's face, she knew she said the wrong thing. Ganika was so offended she set up the dinner and then left the room for the rest of the night. She did not even attend the meal. Yvonne was crestfallen. She felt ill, like the world was collapsing around her.

"I think we should leave," Yvonne said as soon as the meal was completed.

"I agree" said Rajan cooly.

After dinner, Rajan walked Yvonne outside. Immediately Rajan hysterically asked "Why did you say those words. It is so rude. She was insulted."

"I apologize. Please apologize to your mother for me. I spoke incorrectly," said Yvonne. "I guess I was nervous."

"Oh my goodness. I will talk with you later. I have to say bye for now," said Rajan

Rajan had strong feelings for Yvonne, but when it came to him having the personal courage to say what he wanted to his parents and how he felt, he could not do it. His mother's and in turn his family's word on the matter was too important a thing to ignore. They were a large part of his identity and he could not be with Yvonne in a committed relationship if they were not on board.

Within India there were many different traditions, and habits of courting that affected how Yvonne and Rajan dated. For Anglo-Indians it was generally accepted that most people would choose a person of the opposite sex, of a similar age, and a similar race. They would first date that person and then they would marry. But in the native Indian culture the boy's or girl's parents typically arranged whom the child would even consider for marriage.

Without haste, after they left, Rajan's mother, Ganika sat down and wrote a letter to the matchmaker expressing the criteria for a good match to her son: She must be of our religion, must be educated, she must be of our caste and traditions, speak our language well, and eat our food, and her financial and social status must be highly acceptable as well.

It took many years before Yvonne recovered from the break-up of her only Love.

From Boarding School to Convent

Yvonne felt now that all she had were her friends and her job. She sat in her room night after night trying to go over what went wrong with her and Rajan, how she landed where she was, and how it all started.

Thinking back

Yvonne started in a boarding school and stayed right up until 17 years old and then she finished her Cambridge High School studies.

Yvonne would come home in the summer, which started around April 15th and lasted until about June 15th. From the age of 5 to 13, during those 2 months, she returned to her grandmother's house, going only occasionally to spend time with her mother, father, and brothers.

"Nana, I'm home," a young 13-year old voice called out.

"Where have you been Yvonne?" asked Florence, Yvonne's grandmother.

"I went to see Pamela, Iris and Jessie," said Yvonne. These women were some of her close friends from school. Iris Goodman was one of her best friends. *Iris went on to marry Air Marshal Malcolm Wollen who became somewhat of a hero within the Indian Armed forces.*

"You have just been home a few days from school and you still have not seen your father. Go now for dinner with him and your brothers."

"I will Nana, but my friends are going off to a dance tomorrow night. I really need some new clothes."

"Yvonne, you are too young to go to dances. Now go," said Florence

"Nana, I am not too young. I'm almost 13 years old," said Yvonne. "I was wondering if you can take me shopping." Florence looked at her granddaughter with a knowing glance. She wanted to say yes, but wanted Yvonne to do a few things for her as well. Florence thought maybe a little parental leveraging was necessary. Florence typically bought all Yvonne's clothes, food, and toiletries and when school started up once again, she purchased things for her to use at the boarding school as well.

"Okay, you go to dinner with the family," said Florence and I'll make sure that we go out this week for 1 special dress."

"Oh, thank you Nana," Yvonne said smiling.

As she grew into a teenager, the relationship changed between Florence and Yvonne as it does between a teenager and a parent. For Florence it became very difficult. Yvonne grew into an individual who had unique ideas, feelings and perceptions on the world she lived in, as well as how to be treated, and how to treat others. She wanted her grandmother to recognize and respect these feelings.

The teenage rift between Yvonne and her grandmother grew so large that one day Yvonne announced that she was going back to her mother's house to live and never coming back. Florence looked in her eyes and knew that one day this day would come, but she was hoping it would not be like this.

Yvonne stopped living at her grandmother's house when she was 16 years old and it was then that she got to know her brothers' characters and her family's dynamics a little better. It is then she realized how important it was to help them.

In her 16th year, Yvonne went back to school again for her last year at **Jesus and Mary's** school. This time she had a new attitude. She wanted to take on more responsibility and be seen as more mature. At 18 she finished up at the Jesus and Mary's high school, and then graduated to St. Mary's Training school for girls in Poona, India. She was at St. Mary's training college from age 19 to 23.

The St. Mary's school had a long history of academic excellence since its establishment in 1866. Although steeped in tradition, it was unique in the way it kept abreast of the new trends in education and responded to the changing needs of children. Yvonne learned and eventually taught the Montessori method at the school.

St. Mary's School was run by the Sisters of the Community of St. Mary the Virgin, an Anglican order based in Wantage, England. In their hands the School was one of continuous progress and growth.

Yvonne took classes at the training college and also taught children at the secondary school. Since both boys and girls could attend the school, a family friend, had gone there as well when he was her age.

She learned to be a teacher at St. Mary's and since it was a finishing school, she also learned several other important things including etiquette and about respecting the needs of others.

While she was learning how to teach, she had to also work at the school. She went to school in the morning and had a paid internship as a teacher in the afternoon. She only earned about 175 rupees per week, but was able to use that money to pay for her own boarding and help out her mother occasionally.

It was a coveted position, and Yvonne hoped it would lead to a full-time teaching job later.

Years later she would tell her younger brother the back story of how she got the job at the school. "The only reason I got that job was because Mum was very friendly with the doctor who helped deliver us in the hospital."

"Who was that?" asked Gerald.

"It was Dr. Schmoock. She was living in Kirkee and working in the nursing home (maternity hospital)," said Yvonne.

"Was I delivered by Dr. Schmoock?" asked Gerald.

"George, Carlyle, Reggie, Colin, and you and I actually were all delivered by Dr. Schmoock," said Yvonne.

"Yes, She was in Bombay and Kirkee and then moved to Poona," said Yvonne. "She was so friendly with Mother. Do you know she also loved music and started teaching it at St. Mary's?"

"Anyway, she had a lot of influence in getting me into **St. Mary's school** to do my studies, and also in me getting a job at the convent," said Yvonne. "This Dr. Schmook was critical in making that happen. St. Mary's is one of the best schools in India and you know we didn't have the money to pay full tuition."

"Mum didn't pay a rupee?" asked Gerald to Yvonne.

"No," said Yvonne. "How could they? Papa and Mum are not good at saving money,"

It is graduation day.

"I am the first one in the family to graduate from an Intermediate college," Yvonne said proudly to her Mother Superior on her graduation day, as her brothers and cousins looked on. Two of Yvonne's brothers went for free to Jesus and Mary's convent up to 2nd grade, then once they moved on to an all boy's school her parents were required to pay full tuition. Two of her other brothers ended up having truancy problems again and again, until one day they dropped out—never finishing high school. Only Reggie, Dolly's youngest son went on to finish High School, then eventually onto the armed forces.

Yvonne always thought about how she could help her brothers. She felt forever responsible for each of them, and later when her father died, her feelings of responsibility expanded to include her mother.

After finishing college at St. Mary's in 1953, Yvonne entered a career of teaching. Eventually she went on to teach at the **Breach Candy School**, a school in the very wealthy area of Bombay where Germans, Swiss, and other Europeans lived.

The school, located on Cumballa Hill near the port area, sat adjacent to the ocean. Each day, students, teachers, or nuns walked by the ocean for a morning or afternoon break.

After her friendship with Rajan ended, Yvonne moved on. The cloud had dissapated.

She arrived at Breach Candy School when she was 23 years old and stayed there 6 more years. She would call it her fullest 6 years; a time in her life when most women would have been married or starting a family, but instead she wanted to focus on teaching children. She spent 5 to 6 years at the day school run by nuns and a set of rigid rules to teach by. After work, she no longer commuted back to her mother's or grand-mother's house, but to a dormitory-like room at Villa Theresa. Villa Theresa was a well-respected Catholic woman's hostel in the heart of Bombay, adjacent to Breach Candy. The Breach Candy School was run by a British headmistress called Mrs. Adcock, while the hostel was run by nuns. This is the backdrop for Yvonne's life where she lived and she taught for six years.

After work each day she went home to a loving and safe environment surrounded by friends at Villa Theresa. She would go to sleep, wake up and attend a mandatory, early mass, and then eat breakfast with her friends, who were also staying at the hostel. Some Christian Goans lived there, but primarily Anglo-Indian woman stayed at Villa Theresa. During the weekends she would do Tony perms and go on picnics and attend horse races. Although Breech Candy and Villa Theresa were governed by the strict rules of the English nuns, she managed to break away Friday and Saturday nights with her many friends and attend dances and parties, sometimes not coming back till early in the morning.

Deciding to Become
Part of the Change

India was different in kind from the rest of the Empire — British for so long that it had become part of the national consciousness, so immense that it really formed, with Britain itself, the second focus of a dual power. If much of the Empire was a blank in British minds, India meant something to everybody, from the Queen herself with her Hindu menservants to the humblest family whose ne'er-do-well brother, long before, had sailed away to lose himself in the barracks of Cawnpore. India was the brightest gem, the Raj, part of the order of things: to a people of the drizzly north, the possession of such a country was like some marvel in the house, a caged phoenix perhaps, or the portrait of some fabulously endowed if distant relative. India appealed to the British love of pageantry and fairy-tale, and to most people the destinies of the two countries seemed not merely intertwined, but indissoluble.[12] (James Morris, Penguin 1979)

At the height of its glory, the British Empire encompassed nearly a quarter of the earth's land mass and a quarter of its population. Of all its possessions, none was more precious than India, the 'jewel in the crown' of Victoria's Empire.

Yvonne in the meantime, learned the British way and then learned how to teach the British way. The 23-year old Anglo-Indian woman started work as a teacher in 1952. While at the Breach Candy school she helped the nuns and taught the children to read, write and do arithmetic. When Yvonne first started communicating to co-workers and adults she cringed at the thought of saying something incorrectly to others, but as she became a young adult at the Breach Candy school she learned that she had to say what was on her mind if she was going to get what she needed done. Also, Mother Teresa's teachings also had an influence on her and the Anglo-Indian community at that time. Yvonne's friends and she would listen to the radio for anything they could find out about Mother Teresa's activity in India.

After work each day she went home to Villa Theresa. Although like a dormitory, the young woman went out with her friends to dances and more. She had dozens of Anglo-Indian friends enthusiastic to go out at night, dine with her, and share her thoughts and aspirations.

But as the years went by many of Yvonne's good friends left to go to England or Australia or married other Anglo-Indian men who worked the railway, or were in the military and moved on to another city across the Indian landscape. Yvonne also thought about going to England and Australia, but she had also read and heard stories about America and day-dreamed about going there as well.

Her more British friends and cousins, were ready to leave India after the political situation had reached its pinnacle and attitudes changed toward the British.

Attitudes had changed in just the few short years she grew from that naive teenager to now, a woman mature enough to know she was nearing spinsterhood. Every week she heard of another Anglo-Indian woman or man in her circle leaving India and migrating to a far away land. The primary destination for most of these people was the United Kingdom. Did she want to go to England or Ireland? Maybe, but who would be able to take care of her mother and father?

She also loved it here in India for many reasons; the number one being that it was her home: the familiar sounds and smells, the tastes of curry and Biryani, the way children played and talked with each other. If she went somewhere else, all would be different.

People moved away for many reasons; one was fear. Anglo-Indian men feared that mothers, sisters or daughters would be hurt or humiliated in some way in this new post-independent reality. Stories and rumors ran rampant. Radio programs spoke of and films showed the unrest every week. It was difficult to escape the stories, and the rumors had become a way of communicating. They needed direction and guidance.

The Anglo-Indians relied on leaders in their community to help them find that direction. One of those leaders was Frank Anthony, who Dolly was acquainted with and Yvonne met once when she was a young girl. Frank Anthony was Colonel Sir Henry Gidney's successor. Gidney for years had represented the small Anglo-Indian minority within India with great respect, but as he grew older and frailer, he needed a helping hand to lead the cause. Gidney took Anthony under his wing and helped prepare him for the inevitable future, and the political and economic unrest felt by the Anglo-Indian community. The community owed its position in the country entirely to the vocal regional representatives of the Anglo-Indian associations. After Anthony elevated to a leadership position within the All-India Anglo-Indian Association, he was nominated by the Viceroy in August 1942 as the community's sole representative in what was then the Central Legislative Assembly. He was also nominated as a member of the National Defense Council, which helped direct India's war effort. Before Gidney the community's representatives were an appendage of the European Group in the Central Legislature, and politically hung on to the coat tails of that group. Under Frank Anthony's young spirit, the community followed a more goal-oriented approach[13]. It had fallen upon Anthony, to find a place for the community in the New India. For him it was a huge responsibility and huge burden to represent a group that was losing people and losing faith, but loved and were loyal to India.

Anthony gave speeches, attended conferences, held meetings, wrote letters and met one on one with British and Indian officials and members of the community in order to meet the goals and desires of the Anglo-Indian community. One significant goal was just to be recognized as a significant entity within the political landscape. Before long he had the strength of the community behind him. He had seen the leaders of the association go from a point of alliance with the British, facing the Opposition party to the unusual event where he was a nominated member to the front rank of the Opposition party in India's parliament.

Speaking on a pivotal Finance Bill in March 1943, he castigated the English government for the discrimination which it continued to practice against the community. He pointed out the differential pay scales and allowances that were offered to European commissioned officers vs. Indian commissioned officers, and how this racial discrimination translated into economic practice. "...the better educated sons have got the reduced scales of pay because they have refused to deny their parentage or their Community (that they are Anglo-Indian)... If a man lies and makes a false declaration, they pay him more: if a man has the courage of his convictions, they penalize him by giving him a lower wage...As I have said 99.9% of the British Emergency commissioned officers who are domiciled in India are Anglo-Indians... they are drawn from the same cultural and economic stratum as the Indian Commissioned Officers....It is this policy that has adversely affected and emasculated the Anglo-Indian Community," Anthony went on saying. Over and over, and year after year Anthony tried to fight for equality between the British and Indians for the Anglo-Indian's sake. But as much as he tried, he received bitter disappointment.

When the war ended in August 1945, Viceroy Lord Wavell decided to hold a political conference in Simla, to which he invited Muslim League and Congressional representatives.

A representative from the Anglo-Indian Association had been excluded from the Simla Conference, making Anthony furious and Anglo-Indian community full of disappointment, seeing that they may be denied what Indian leaders are prepared to grant. The obvious conclusion was that all were compelled to draw from the Simla conference exclusion was that the British Government was not prepared to go out of its way to do anything to assist the Anglo-Indian community. Rumors spread rapidly that not even the association had power now.

However, Anthony and the Association continued with their efforts on behalf of the community.

For the moment, Frank Anthony and the Association worked toward constitutional changes and to integrate verbiage into formal law against discrimination, and making sure Anglo-Indians were getting notoriety and credit for their achievements. By spring of 1946, Anthony had been recognized as the "able" spokesperson, and the Anglo-Indian community had been understood to have entered the "nationalist fold".

Anthony eventually met with India's leaders, including *Gandhiji*. At that time Mahatma Gandhi was staying with what is known as the sweeper colony. He gave Anthony a long and patient visit. At the end of the meeting, Gandhiji asked Anthony, *why does the community want recognition as a separate entity?*

Anthony explained at length that without it, this would mean the destruction of the community. "The Anglo Indians in fact are the only real-racial-cum-linguistic minority in India. Over a period of 300 years we have evolved into a distinctive, homogeneous entity with our own way of life, our culture and our language, English." He pointed out that the Anglo-Indians would regard any de-recognition of our position as a distinctive minority as a blow at our very existence.

Months later, Gandhi, Anthony and others within other minority communities managed to work together. They were moving slowly toward a change that could help everyone.

Even with the fearless Gandhi's tragic death by an assassin, the change came. But by then, many Anglo-Indians did not want to be a part of that change.

The Exodus

For the most part, the British left first, and then the Anglo-Indians. People left by the thousands to the UK, Australia, Canada and America, causing the UK and others to eventually institute Immigration Acts, which placed restrictions on the number of people entering those countries. Alfred Devereux's family returned to England, while others in the family went to Australia and others to Canada. Evelyn Devereux Rixson and her husband also followed into the countryside of England and then to the Isle of White, while some of her children joined the couple in England and some went straight to Australia.

Frank Anthony writes in his Story of the Anglo Indian Community: "Undoubtedly, the exodus has weakened the community not only numerically but also in respect of its social and economic texture." He estimated that about 50,000 Anglo-Indians had migrated since independence through to the early 1970s: 25,000 to the United Kingdom, 5 to 10,000 to Australia, and 5 to 10,000 to New Zealand, Canada and America. [14]

Yvonne wanted to follow suit, but after being a trained teacher, she was finally managing to stand on her own two feet and making a decent living. Besides the daytime work at Breach Candy School, she was offered the opportunity to take on private tutoring for the many Anglo-Indian parents that wanted their children to have a better start at English and Arithmetic. And what better way but by an English bred, Anglo-Indian teacher who also by that time knew Hindi fairly well. With her income saved, she could have easily gone to Australia, but then who would have taken care of her mother Dolly and father James? Her brothers had since left for positions in business or the armed forces, and with her grandmother gone; she was the only one to be able to send money home regularly every month, which she gladly did for her parents.

From Convent
to Marriage

Into the early 1950s the Villa Theresa convent school on Cumballa Hill in Bombay was an institution that still held Roman Catholic nuns and taught the British way, but in an environment where India was growing less of a British colony. They needed new nuns to teach-- who were well-liked, well-educated and knew Hindi. It was a natural assumption that Yvonne would be a candidate—especially to be a nun. She lived in the hostel of Villa Theresa for 3 years before the Nuns started talking about converting her to become a Nun herself.

"A 27-year old single girl is no longer a girl, she is a woman, and I don't think of marrying age any more," said Mother Superior.

"Yes, you are right. Who would marry her? These Indian men marry so young and the men who are older I wouldn't trust," said sister Grace.

"And she has no money or direct family that she is close with in Australia or England to go over there and live with, as so many have now gone. Her mother and father are living in Poona and her brothers and cousins are scattered throughout India," said Mother Superior to the sister.

"She is self-sufficient, strong, and well-liked," said Sister Grace. "I think Yvonne will like the idea of being a Nun. You will see."

Yvonne had other dreams.

She looked at herself in the mirror. Her thick black eye-lashes framed her deep, dark brown eyes. Her complexion was creamy white with flushed cheeks, rosy lips, and straight white teeth showed when she smiled. Her tiny waist could fit within the circle of large, rugged, masculine hands. She had beauti-ful, long dark black hair, which she wore to the middle of her back or in a neat pile on the top of her head. Her figure was petite and men found her attractive. She was over the crushing breakup of Rajan and moved on. She was ready for a more sub-stantial relationship now and made sure her friends knew. She was ready for marriage.

Yvonne's friend Shanti had the match made even before she told Yvonne. Shanti was married to a seaman Victor and they invited Yvonne over one night to introduce her to a mutual friend.

Shanti was a smart and spirited woman about the same age as Yvonne. She and Yvonne were living in a rapidly chang-ing culture and had more options and ideas on how best to find a mate. Due to failed attempts at romance, Yvonne finally agreed to find her husband the old-fashioned way--- via an arranged marriage. When she told her friend, Shanti couldn't wait to start.

"Shanti, you know that I have had a few dates over the years after Rajan, but they ended awkwardly and I felt under constant pressure to move it along," said Yvonne.

"Yvonne, those nuns are going to try and marry you off to God," Shanti said laughing. "We have to do something about this soon. Why hasn't your mother arranged anything?" asked Shanti.

"My mother? She doesn't know anyone, and anyway, my parents have no money to give to a match maker or for a dowry," said Yvonne.

Yvonne, thinking that she was nearing the deadline for starting a family, agreed to a match that Shanti or her other friends would like to try and arrange.

Finally, the night of Yvonne's "blind date" at Shanti's house came to pass. When Marco Antonio Velasquez arrived, the first thing Yvonne noticed was his strong Columbian accent, which made it difficult to understand him. But very quickly she saw his warm, friendly eyes and that he was very handsome and polite. She agreed without hesitation, to go out with him on a separate date the next day. Yvonne was 28 years old, when she fell in love with 41-year old Marco. He was a Merchant Marine, who had traveled around the world on commercial vessels, part of the time on the National Maritime Union's ships.

A whirlwind romance unfolded and within 5 days the two were engaged.

Mother Superior was shocked and furious, "Absolutely not. You don't even know this man well enough or his family. He is in his 40s and probably has a wife in every port!"

"Mother, I can assure you. He is not married. He is in love with me and I am sure I don't want to be a Nun. I want to marry him," said Yvonne.

"We will not marry you here," Mother Superior said emphatically.

"You will not marry me here? But I have worked here and given so much to this church Mother," said Yvonne.

"Where will you go if he leaves you? Instead, if you become a nun you will see that your life here in India will be very fruitful," said Mother Superior.

Yvonne paused. It had crossed her mind as an alternative for quite a while, but knew it would not satisfy her. "Thank you, but that is not for me. I am sure that I want to marry him. We are going to America." Yvonne painstakingly explained to Mother Superior, the church's priest and the other nuns who tried to convince her to stay.

When Marco heard that the nuns and priests were giving Yvonne such a hard time he was furious. He developed a plan and told it to Yvonne the next day. Marco asked Yvonne to meet him in "3 months time in Calcutta", where he would dock, come off the ship and marry her properly—in a church. Yvonne was not happy about the fact that her mother, father or brothers were not going to be able to attend the wedding, but came to understand that it was probably the only way. He in turn begged her to try and make it work. She eventually wrote a letter and told him "Yes, I will be there."

Upon telling her mother Dolly about the plans for the approaching marriage, Dolly agreed and contacted her brother, Jack Devereux. Jack was now an executive manager at the Jessup car manufacturing company in Calcutta and doing very well. He and his wife Ivy agreed to attend. They arrived early to meet Yvonne at the Calcutta airline. They would be the couple's only witnesses and family attending.

Marco arrived early at the church, with a friend from the ship joyful and excited, dressed in a dark suit and ready to be married. The young couple embraced and proceeded to handle the formalities of the license. Uncle Jack walked her down the aisle and smiled to Marco as he gave her away. Aunty Ivy and Joan, her daughter, were witnesses, as well as Marco's friend from the ship.

The couple married in the heart of Calcutta as her grandmother Evelyn had nearly 40 years prior.

The next week Marco sailed off on the large commercial shipping vessel headed towards Africa and then to America, where he would prepare his home for both of them to start a family. My mother left India for America a few weeks later to meet up with him, which was in the spring of 1958.

As she left for the Bombay airport, she heard a tune playing in the background somewhere on a radio. ...*Send her victorious. Happy and glorious. Long to reign over us. God save the Queen...*

In the end, she was not known as Indian, but a citizen of India—a legal native of India. As she left, her heart had loyalty and patriotism for the one country she had always known and loved.

Postscript

Yvonne and Marco came to America and lived a fulfilling life of gentle rewards in New York City. They started a family of their own and within 5 years had three children, which were named—Indira, Anil, and Sonina. They were married for 37 years, until Marco's death at age 78.

Overall, approximately 6,000 Asian Indians immigrated to the United States post Independence, between 1947 and 1965. This was considered the first wave of immigration and included many Anglo-Indians. Yvonne Velasquez (nee LeStyne) was part of that first wave of that early immigration after Independence. For this group, the transition may have been the hardest.

From about 1965 forward, a second important wave of Indian immigration began, started by a change in U.S. immigration law that lifted prior restrictions. Of equal importance was that after Jawaharlal Nehru died (1964), and the general Indian election took place (1966) more fuel was added to the flames and a different exodus had started. Between 1965 and 1974, Indian immigration to the United States increased at a rate greater than that from almost any other country. Almost 40 percent of all Indian immigrants who entered the United States in the decades after 1965 arrived on student or exchange visitor visas, and in some instances with their family and other dependents. This wave of immigrants was very different from the earlier Indian immigrants—Indians that emigrated after 1965 were predominantly urban, professional, highly educated and quickly engaged in gainful employment in many U.S. cities. Many had prior exposure to Western society and their transition to the United States was therefore relatively smoother. [15]

A few years after Yvonne came to America, she received a letter from a friend telling her that her father James died of a heart attack in India. My mother was heartbroken that she could not be there for her mother and was overwhelmed by feelings of sadness. Eventually, the feelings of sadness morphed into worry for her mother's well being. So it was then, that my mother saved money for my Grandmother Dorothy LeStyne's passage to America. My Grandmother arrived in New York and came to live with us. But clearly, from her stories, she was never as happy as she was in India. She disliked the American ways for many different reasons, but managed to live a comfortable life with advantages and functional amenities here. She helped to take care of her 3 grandchildren after school until Yvonne came home from her job at the bank every day.

Evelyn and John Rixson moved back to England in the 1930's. Evelyn's son Jack Devereux, his wife Ivy, and their daughter Joan all followed to England to live with their other friends and relatives, about the same time Yvonne left to go to America.

Yvonne's brothers Gerald and Reggie eventually followed her to America. Gerald LeStyne was working at a commercial business in India for many years while his family grew. He saved up enough money for his passage and Yvonne sponsored him in 1974. After a year of working in New York, Gerald brought his wife Virginia and his children Tyrone and Sabrina to America.

In 1957, Reginald LeStyne joined the Indian Air Force and held a career with the air force for many years. When his term was over it was about 1978. Yvonne wrote to him and his wife Della and told them of the educational opportunities here in America for his children and that if he wanted she could sponsor him and he could come to America. When he came out of the Air force, he was given a lump sum of money which he used to bring the entire family over, all at once in 1979.

George LeStyne and his wife chose to stay with their family in Delhi, India, where their children eventually grew up and started their own families. My mother sent money several times to the family, still trying to participate in her Anglo-Indian family from afar, and then in 2000 she bought a house for George and his wife, and their extended family to live a more comfortable life.

About 22 years later my mother Yvonne and I went back to India to visit her Anglo-Indian relatives and friends. I was 16-years old. She returned to India with a silent expectation that the country was still hers —that she could recapture its essence and it could fulfill something it so many years ago had fulfilled in her. But what she found was that India had simply changed. Those older Anglo-Indians from the British Raj era who still remained were but merely a shell of what they once were. All were living very poorly compared to how they lived 40 years prior, but still their joyful smiles shown and she could see that they had adapted. They did not want to be anywhere else but where they were.

The children of her Anglo-Indian friends and relatives were completely accepting of the new India, and yet some still yearned to go to America or England or Australia. But, for the many in that younger generation the thought was more that they would reach their goals on Indian soil. They were making plans to stand on their own—hopeful plans with great reach and fervor.

The End

Timeline Highlights

Year	Historical Event	Details
1500s	Mogul Empire grows	The rule of the Mogul Empire begins in India, unifying much of south India with northern India for the first time.
1600s	East India Company; Queen Elizabeth I granted a charter to the East India Company and established trading posts in Bombay, Calcutta, and Madras	Eager to gain access to India's spices, rice, silk, tea and jewels, Holland, Great Britain and France establish key trading posts in India; Mogul Emperor Shah Jahan begins construction of the Taj Mahal; East India Company is founded followed by a trading network into the next century
1757	Battle of Plassey (Part of Seven Years War" in Europe)	British troops in the service of the East India Company (EIC) defeat the French and the Indians who support the French troops. As a result, British power and the power of the EIC expand dramatically. Battle of Plassey is judged to be one of the pivotal battles leading to the eventual formation of the British Empire in India.

1857-1858	1858 War of Independence; Government of India Act	India's First War of Independence, termed Sepoy Riots by the British was an attempt to unite India against the invading British and to restore power to the Mogul emperor Bahadur Shah (who was exiled afterwards); The British overthrow the Moguls and take control of India; In August 1858 the British crown assumed control of India from the East India Company; English was made the official language and several traditional Hindu customs were outlawed. Political power was transferred from the East India Company directly to the British Crown; EIC was dissolved.
1877	British Raj = British rule in India	Queen Victoria crowned as the Empress of India.
1885	Indian National Congress	The Indian National Congress created (also known as the Congress Party / INC) and becomes the major political party in India and eventually the leading party toward the Independence Movement in its struggle against the British Empire.

1893 to 1901	*Jungle Book* and *Kim* by Rudyard Kipling published	*Jungle Book* is about a boy raised by wolves in the Indian Jungle; *Kim* takes place during the backdrop of the political conflict between Russia and Britain in Central Asia.
1902	White Australia Policy activated	Introduced to restrict further Indian immigration, except for Anglo-Celtic colonials (lasted till 1973)
1915	Gandhi begins resistance work in India	After studying law in Britain and fighting for Indian rights in South Africa, Mohandas Gandhi launches a campaign of nonviolent resistance against British rule in India. Gandhi is called Mahatma, meaning "Great Soul."
1916	Gandhi campaigns	Gandhi led nationwide campaigns for the decrease of poverty, for the liberation of women, for brotherhood amongst different religious and ethnic groups, for an end to untouchability and caste discrimination, and for the economic self-sufficiency of the nation, but above all for Swaraj—the independence of India from foreign domination.
1919	Amritsar Massacre	An incident in which British troops fired on a crowd of unarmed Indian protesters (including women and children) killing a large number. It left a permanent scar on Indo-British relations.

1920-22	Mahatma Gandhi's noncooperation movement	The non-violent protests against the British in India consisted of the resignations of titles; the boycott of government educational institutions, the courts, government service, foreign goods, and elections; and the eventual refusal to pay taxes. The movement marks the transition of Indian nationalism from a middle-class to a mass basis.
1922	Gandhi imprisoned	Gandhi was sentenced to six years for civil disobedience but was released after serving two.
1924	*A Passage to India* by E. M. Forster published	A novel by English author E. M. Forster set against the backdrop of the British Raj and the Indian independence movement in the 1920s

Year	Historical Event
1929	U.S. stock market collapses leading to worldwide economic depression (Great Depression). *The Remaking of Village India* by F.L. Brayne published (London, Bombay) **Yvonne LeStyne born – July 1929 to Dorothy Devereux and James LeStyne.**
1930	Indian salt march - Gandhi and thousands of other Indians angered by the imposition of a salt tax start out on a massive "Salt March".
1931	*A Farewell to India by* Edward John Thompson published

1932	Gandhi begins a "fast unto death" to protest the British government's treatment of India's lowest caste "untouchables" whom Gandhi calls Harijans ---- "God's children."
1933	Anglo-Indian actress Merle Oberon plays Anne Boleyn in the film - *The Private Life of Henry VIII*
1934	Adolf Hitler becomes leader of Germany; *Burmese Days* by George Orwell published
1936	Edward VIII, King of England abdicates after 325 days; George VI becomes King of England
1939	The All India Forward Bloc, a leftwing nationalist political party in India emerges as a faction within the Indian National Congress led by Subhas Chandra Bose; Britain and France declare war on Germany
1940	Battle of Britain – British air victory prevents German invasion
1941	The Japanese bomb Pearl Harbor, Hawaii; U.S. enters WWII.
1945	Mussolini assassinated; Hitler commits suicide; Germany Surrenders; United States dropped atomic bombs on Hiroshima and Nagasaki; WWII ends
1946	Peace conference opens in Paris; Republic of Hungary proclaimed; Jordan gains independence
1947	India gains independence (decolonization begins); Partition of India takes place --Two dominions created India (Hindu) and Pakistan (Muslim); Dispute erupts between India and Pakistan over Kashmir— state ceded to India; Burma gains independence
1948	Mahatma Gandhi assassinated at a prayer meeting by Hindu extremist; Ceylon becomes a self-governing dominion; State of Israel declared and War between Israel and Arab League begins;

1949	Indian constitution is adopted. Many thousands of people start migrating from India and Pakistan to Britain and other countries (through the 1950s) to settle there for good.
1950	Indian constitution is adopted and India becomes a federal republic within the Commonwealth; U.S. in Korean War (until 1953)
1952	Elizabeth II becomes queen of Britain; First national election in India—J. Nehru elected prime minister
1955	In 1955 the Indian National Congress adopted socialism as its policy. Thus leaders like Yagee and Singh then proposed that as the Congress had become a socialist party, the Forward Bloc (Marxist) ought to merge with it.
1957	Dwight D. Eisenhower in office; European Economic Community formed (European common market); Suez Canal re-opens for all shipping *Yvonne leaves India with her husband Marco to go to America*
1958	U.S. Launches first space satellite – space race begins
1960	J.F. Kennedy elected president (youngest and first Catholic President)
1961	Britain begins application to join European Economic Community; South Africa becomes a republic
1962	First live TV broadcasts between U.S and Europe
1963	JFK assassinated; Lyndon B. Johnson takes office
1964	U.S. involvement in Vietnam War increases; Civil Rights Act becomes law
1965	India and Pakistan go to war over Kashmir; Winston Churchill dies;
1966	Indira Gandhi is elected Prime Minister of India and one of the first women to lead a nation.

1969	Richard Nixon takes office; American astronauts land on the moon; Hare Krishna movement gains momentum in America.
1971	East Pakistan becomes independent as Bangladesh after civil war and intervention by India
1972	Ceylon becomes republic of Sri Lanka; Britain takes over direct rule of Northern Ireland
1973	U.S. withdraws troops from Vietnam
1974	Nixon forced to resign after Watergate scandal
1980	The world population has more than doubled since Yvonne's birth
1981	Ronald Reagan takes office; 52 American Hostages captured by Iran in the seizure of U.S. embassy in Teheran, were released and returned to the U.S.; AIDS name given to a disease affecting 26 patients
1983	India wins the cricket world cup
1985	Gorbachev becomes Soviet leader
1989	End of Cold war between U.S. and Russia; Communist rule ends in Bulgaria, Hungary and Czechoslovakia
1990	Communist monopoly of power ends in the U.S.S.R
1992	Bill Clinton elected president
1998	India tests its first nuclear weapon
2000-2013	9-11 bombing of NY Twin Towers; Barack Obama (first African American U.S. President) gets elected; India's population exceeds 1 billion
2014	Yvonne Velasquez (nee LeStyne) celebrates 85th birthday with extended family (New Jersey)

Selected Bibliography

Anthony, Frank. Britain's Betrayal in India: The Story of the Anglo Indian Community. UK: Simon Wallenberg Press, (1964, 2007).

Bhatia, Tej K. Colloquial Hindi, London: Routledge 1996.

Cooke, Jean and Ann Kramer, Theodore Rowland-Entwistle. History's Timeline: A 40,000 Year Chronology of Civilization. London: 1981.

Copeland, Lewis and Lawrence W. Lamm. The World's Great Speeches, 3rd Ed. New York: Dover Publications, 1973

Dalrymple, William. The Last Mughal: The Fall of a Dynasty, Delhi, 1857.

Dewey, Clive. Anglo Indian Attitudes – The Mind of the Indian Civil Service. London: Bloomsbury Academic, (1993, 2003).

Harrison, Mark. Public Health in British India: Anglo-Indian Preventive Medicine 1859-1914. Cambridge: Cambridge University Press, 1994.

Johnson, Alan. Out of Bounds: Anglo-Indian Literature and the Geography of Displacement, Univ of Hawaii, 2011.

Kagan, Donald, Steven Ozment, Frank M. Turner. Western Heritage, 2nd Ed., Since 1648, Macmillan Publishing Co., New York, 1983.

Gandhi, Rajmohan. Gandhi: The Man, His People, and the Empire, 2008.

Giridharadas, Anand. India Calling. New York: Henry Holt and Company, 2011.

Herman, Arthur. Gandhi & Churchill: The Epic Rivalry that Destroyed an Empire and Forged Our Age, 2009.

Holmes, John Haynes. Mahatma Gandhi His Own Story, C.F. Andrews (Editor), 1930.

Lerner, Robert, Standish Meacham, Edward McNall Burns, Western Civilization: The History and Their Culture, 13th Ed. WW Norton & Company, New York, 1998.

Mack, E.C., *Public Schools and British Opinion - Since 1860*, Westpoint, CT, 1971.

MAHMOOD, SYED. "A History of English Education in India (1781-1893)." Archive.org. M. A.-O. College, Aligarh, n.d. Web. Nov. 2014.

Morgan, Susan. Bombay Anna. Berkley, Los Angeles: University of California Press, 2008.

Morris, James (Jan). Pax Britannica: The Climax of an Empire. Penguin Books Ltd, 1979.

Matteo, Sonina. *Yvonne Velasquez (nee LeStyne)* Interview Notes/Personal interviews. 2000-2014.

Savage, Richard. A Fascinating Traitor. An Anglo-Indian Story, 1897.

Syed Mahmood. History of English Education in India (1781-1893), Honorary Secretary of the M.A.-O College, Aligarh.

Telephony Publishing Company, *Telephony*, The American Telephone Journal, Chicago, 1910.

Von Tunzelmann, Alex, <u>Indian Summer: The Secret History of the End of an Empire</u>, Henry Holt and Company, New York, 2007.

Wilkinson, Philip, <u>Religions, Visual Reference Guide</u>, Metro Books, New York, 2010.

Wilson, <u>The Domiciled European and Anglo –Indian Race of India</u>, Bombay, 1926.

Yule, Henry & A.C. Burnell, <u>Hobson-Jobson. A Glossary of Colloquial Anglo-Indian Words and Phrases, and of Kindred Terms, Etymological, Historical, Geographical and Discursive.</u> This was an historical dictionary of Anglo-Indian words and terms from Indian languages which came into use during the British rule of India and widely used. (1939, 1996)

The author also utilized miscellaneous articles and data from the following publications and online sources:

World History Project.org

Families in British India Society database (Fibis.org)

Wikipedia online encyclopedia

WikiTree.com

Ancestry.com

The British Library (http://www.bl.uk)

History of India (http://www.historyindia.org)

End Notes

1   "Indian National Association", Wikopedia, 2014, Web. 11 January 2014. <http://en.wikipedia.org/wiki/Indian_ National_Association>, and Alex Von Tunzelmann, Indian Summer: The Secret History of the End of an Empire (New York, Henry Holt and Company, 2007), pp 45-60.

2   "A History of English Education in India (1781-1893)", Archive.org. 2014, Web. November 2014, <https:// archive.org/stream/historyofenglish032043mbp/history-ofenglish032043mbp_djvu.txt>

3   Clive Dewey, Anglo Indian Attitudes – The Mind of the Indian Civil Service, (London, Bloomsbury Academic, 1993); and a "Brief History of India", Naeem Shaikh, May 2013, <https://prezi.com/8slizsofty_c/ brief-history-of-india/>

4   William Dalrymple, The Last Mughal: The Fall of a Dynasty, Delhi 1857; also_Wikipedia (search term 'Kolkata')

5   Donald Kagan, Steven Ozment, Frank M. Turner, Western Heritage, 2nd Ed., Since 1648, Macmillan Publishing Co., New York 1983

6   Rajmohan Gandhi, Gandhi: The Man, His People, and the Empire (2008); Also, Mahatma Gandhi His Own Story, C.F. Andrews (Editor), John Haynes Holmes (1930);

7   Arthur Herman, <u>Gandhi & Churchill: The Epic Rivalry that Destroyed an Empire and Forged Our Age</u> – (2009)

8   Frank Anthony, <u>Britain's Betrayal in India: The Story of the Anglo Indian Community</u> (UK: Simon Wallenberg Press, 2007) p 112.

9   Frank Anthony, <u>Britain's Betrayal in India: The Story of the Anglo Indian Community</u> (UK: Simon Wallenberg Press, 2007) pp 88 to 98.

10   The Thomas Edison Papers, http://edison.rutgers.edu/list.htm; http://nowweknowem.com/2014/01/; Telephony, volume 18, pp 392-393.

11   "Anglo Indians in the IAF", Site created and designed by Group Captain Kapil Bhargava, <http://www.bharat-rakshak.com/IAF/History/1950s/Anglos.html>   (article originally appeared in *INDIAN AVIATION Magazine*)

12   James (Jan) Morris, <u>Pax Britannica: The Climax of an Empire</u>, (Penguin Books Ltd, 1979); Also, Alan Johnson, <u>Out of Bounds: Anglo-Indian Literature and the Geography of Displacement</u> (Univ of Hawaii, 2011), p. 144.

13   Frank Anthony, <u>Britain's Betrayal in India: The Story of the Anglo Indian Community</u> (UK: Simon Wallenberg Press, 2007) pp. 394 to 399.

14   Frank Anthony, <u>Britain's Betrayal in India: The Story of the Anglo Indian Community</u> (UK: Simon Wallenberg Press, 2007) pp. 208, 382 to 384.

15   "Asian Indian Americans, Countries and Their Cultures", Pavri Tinaz < http://www.everyculture.com/multi/A-Br/Asian-Indian-Americans.html>

Appendix:
Photographs and Maps

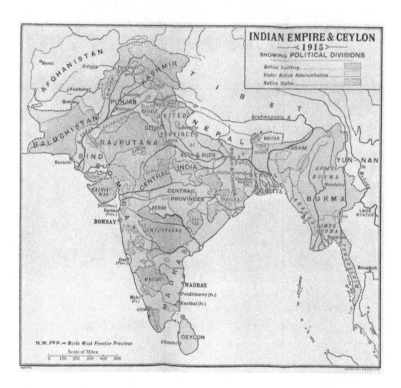

Indian Empire and Ceylon, 1915 (Source: George Philip & Son, Ltd.)

LeStyne Family: (L-R top) Yvonne, Carlyle, Collin, James,
(L-R-bottom) George, Gerald, Dorothy, Reggie

Lady Anne DeQuadros

Sir Michael DeQuadros
K.I.C.G.M

Jane Evelyn Devereux-
Rixson (England Nana)
and John Rixson, India

James LeStyne and Dorothy
Devereux LeStyne with
Yvonne and Carlyle (India)

Florence A. DeQuadros-
LeStyne bathing James, India

The young Florence
DeQuadros, India

Florence DeQuadros LeStyne and George LeStyne
Golden Wedding Anniversary, India

James and Dorothy LeStyne in front of their bungalow, Mount Abu India (Both worked there briefly after the kids left home)

Dorothy, James and Yvonne LeStyne, Kirkee India

Yvonne, 16 years old, India

Yvonne LeStyne, getting ready for a dance. India

Yvonne 4-18-1952, India

Yvonne, India (passport photo)

Yvonne watching over
children from theBreach
Candy School, India

Yvonne's co-workers, teachers,
and nuns at Villa Theresa, India

Yvonne (kneeling-Left) with teachers at Breach
Candy School, 3-18-1955, India

Auntie Kathleen's son, Ivor Stevens upon Graduation
from University (for his Engineering degree)

Jack Devereux

Yvonne, 1957. On vacation
in Nainital India

Yvonne at picnic in Kirkee
India (Botanical Gardens)

Yvonne Velasquez (nee
LeStyne), the year she
arrived in New York City

A young DeQuadros at 16

Jane Evelyn Rixson (far right) and her husband (back). After she returned to England. Sitting with friends McDermotts (reportedly Isle of Wight-where Evelyn and John settled)

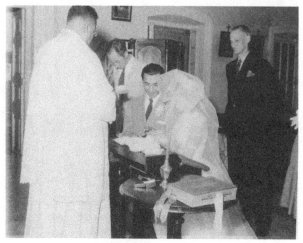

Yvonne and Marco, Wedding Day (Jack Devereux is in black suit in the background)

Marco Velasquez and Yvonne on their wedding day, India

Yvonne with Carlyle (back)
and friend in Kirkee, India

Teachers at Saint Mary's
School. Yvonne (right)

About the Author

Sonina K. Matteo lives with her family in New Jersey, USA. She has worked as a documentation engineer/technical writer and business analyst for over 25 years. She has a background in technical journalism and has published articles for print and online magazines. This is her first book.

Sonina says "My mother's family lived for many years in India while the British ruled. In this story, the Anglo-Indian community is uncovered through my mother's eyes." Thousands of Asian Indians immigrated to England, Australia, Canada, United States, and several more countries post Indian Independence, between 1947 and 1965. This was considered the first wave of immigration and included many Anglo-Indians. Her mother was part of that first wave of immigration after Independence, but was among the last to leave within her community—the Last of that Anglo-Indian group.